COLORADO·CHRISTIAN
COLLEGE

BIBLE PROMISES

Help & Hope for Your
FINANCES

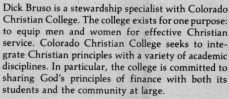

Dick Bruso is a stewardship specialist with Colorado Christian College. The college exists for one purpose: to equip men and women for effective Christian service. Colorado Christian College seeks to integrate Christian principles with a variety of academic disciplines. In particular, the college is committed to sharing God's principles of finance with both its students and the community at large.

The Scriptures instruct us to be faithful stewards of what the Lord has placed in our care. This unique and easy-to-use financial concordance shares God's Word on all areas of finance. Our prayer is that this valuable book will assist you in making wise financial decisions.

by Dick Bruso

BIBLE PROMISES

Help & Hope for Your FINANCES

Here's Life Publishers

Bible Promises
HELP AND HOPE FOR YOUR FINANCES
Dick Bruso

Published by
Here's Life Publishers
P.O. Box 1576, San Bernardino, CA 92402
ISBN 0-89840-075-9
HLP Product No. 950683

Second printing July, 1985
Third printing November, 1985

Printed in the United States of America.

Unless otherwise indicated, Scriptures are taken from the
HOLY BIBLE: NEW INTERNATIONAL VERSION.
Copyright © 1973, 1978 by the International Bible
Society. Used by permission of Zondervan Bible
Publishers. Other quotations are taken from *The Living
Bible* (TLB), © 1971 by Tyndale House Publishers,
Wheaton, Illinois, and used by permission; and the King
James version (KJV).

FOR MORE INFORMATION, WRITE:
L.I.F.E.—P.O. Box A399, Sydney South 2000, Australia
Campus Crusade for Christ of Canada—Box 300, Vancouver, B.C., V6C 2X3, Canada
Campus Crusade for Christ—103 Friar Street, Reading RGI 1EP, Berkshire, England
Lay Institute for Evangelism—P.O. Box 8786, Auckland 3, New Zealand
Great Commission Movement of Nigeria, P.O. Box 500, Jos, Plateau State Nigeria, West Africa
Life Ministry—P.O. Box/Bus 91015, Auckland Park 2006, Republic of South Africa
Campus Crusade for Christ International—Arrowhead Springs, San Bernardino, CA 92414, U.S.A.

Library of Congress Cataloging in Publication Data

Bible. English. New International. Selections.
    1985.
    Bible promises.

    Includes index.
    1. Stewardship, Christian—Biblical teaching.
I. Bruso, Dick, 1943   II. Title. BS391.2.B87   1985   220.5'2   85-62382

To my dear wife, Joann, whose love, encouragement, and sacrifice have helped to make this book a reality and to four other treasures with which God has so richly blessed me—my daughters, Julie-ann, Jackie, Jenny, and Joy.

Contents

ACKNOWLEDGMENTS

My special thanks and great appreciation to:
- Steve Vanden Heuvel, my good friend, who assisted me with the initial research some six years ago and has been very supportive ever since.
- John Bass, Executive Vice-president of the Christian Booksellers Association, who encouraged me early on and gave me my start as a writer via *The Bookstore Journal*.
- Byron MacDonald, my pastor and friend, who spent numerous hours with me in the final editing stages to ensure accuracy in the presentation of God's Word.
- Les Stobbe, my editor, and his assistant, Jean Bryant, for their enthusiasm for this project during its various stages, as well as their patient guidance.

And a very special acknowledgment to:
- Nancy Petrie, my friend, secretary, and office manager, who unselfishly spent many, many months in assuring the successful completion of this book by typing, editing, and providing valuable suggestions and constant encouragement.

INTRODUCTION

Over the decades many fine books have been written on the subject of finance, each in its own way attempting to show the reader how to achieve true and lasting financial success.

Amazingly enough, only one book, written several thousand years ago, contains financial principles that have proven to work *all* the time in *every* situation for *every person*. That book is the Bible—the greatest financial textbook ever written!

I can make this statement with absolute confidence. In the fall of 1978 what began as a six-month project evolved into a six-year adventure in locating and categorizing all the Scriptures referring to finance. To my delight I discovered over 2000 passages on finances and related subjects. After careful and prayerful evaluation of all those passages, I believe the ones chosen for this book, *Help and Hope for Your Finances,* will be the most useful.

As you delve into this biblical guide on finances, you will discover "the words of the Lord are flawless, like silver refined in a furnace of clay, purified seven times" (Psalm 12:6, NIV).

The major topics related to financial matters are listed alphabetically. Then, under each topical heading, the appropriate Scriptures are listed in the order in which they appear in the Bible, for easy reference. Unless otherwise indicated, the New International Version (NIV) has been used throughout. In some instances we have selected only part of a verse and you may want to read these in your own Bible in their entirety. Other versions of the Bible that we have used are *The Living Bible* (TLB) and the King James version (KJV).

The uses of this book are endless! For example, use it:

In counseling others. If you are a pastor, marriage counselor, financial planner, etc., you can locate the appropriate topics quickly and share God's insights as you counsel.

For Bible studies and teaching. Take a particular topic and discuss all the verses that apply; or use this guide as a supplement to other resources on finances.

As an outreach. As a businessman, homemaker, etc., why not give *Help And Hope For Your Finances* to those who have little or no knowledge of God and His Word?

And of course . . .

For personal use. Perhaps you need *help* in investing your money, saving for retirement, or establishing a budget. God's Word has the answer; for "All Scripture is God-breathed and is useful for teaching, rebuking, correcting and training in righteousness, so that the man of God may be thoroughly equipped for every good work" (2 Timothy 3:16, NIV).

If, on the other hand, you are facing financial adversity caused by indebtedness, the loss of your job, or other financial difficulties, do not be discouraged, "for everything that was written in the past was written to teach us, so that through endurance and the encouragement of the Scriptures we might have *hope*" (Romans 15:4, NIV).

As you use this guide, take the time to memorize those Scriptures pertaining to your area of personal concern, letting "the word of Christ dwell in you richly" (Colossians 3:16a, NIV).

Finally, as you apply God's Word in your life, remember that the key to success in any matter, including finances, is contentment. As Paul so beautifully states, "I know what it is to be in need, and I know what it is to have plenty. I have learned the secret of being content in any and every situation, whether well fed or hungry, whether living in plenty or in want. I can do everything through Him who gives me strength" (Philippians 4:12,13, NIV).

Yes, God will provide true contentment in your life and His Word will give you all the "help and hope for your finances" you will ever need.

Handling
ADVERSITY
(See also Security, Worry)

Psalm 16

8 I have set the Lord always before me. Because He is at my right hand, I will not be shaken.

Psalm 23

4 I will fear no evil, for you are with me; your rod and your staff, they comfort me.

Psalm 27

1 The Lord is my light and my salvation—whom shall I fear? The Lord is the stronghold of my life—of whom shall I be afraid? 2 When evil men advance against me to devour my flesh, when my enemies and my foes attack me, they will stumble and fall.

14 Wait for the Lord; be strong and take heart and wait for the Lord.

Psalm 34

19 A righteous man may have many troubles, but the Lord delivers him from them all.

Psalm 46

1 God is our refuge and strength, an ever present help in trouble.

Ecclesiastes 7

14 Enjoy prosperity whenever you can, and when hard times strike, realize that God gives one as well

as the other—so that everyone will realize that nothing is certain in this life (TLB).

John 16

33 I have told you these things, so that in me you may have peace. In this world you will have trouble. But take heart! I have overcome the world.

Romans 5

1 Therefore, since we have been justified through faith, we have peace with God through our Lord Jesus Christ, 2 through whom we have gained access by faith into this grace in which we now stand. And we rejoice in the hope of the glory of God. 3 Not only so, but we also rejoice in our sufferings, because we know that suffering produces perseverance; 4 perseverance, character; and character, hope. 5 And hope does not disappoint us, because God has poured out His love into our hearts by the Holy Spirit, whom He has given us.

Romans 8

28 And we know that in all things God works for the good of those who love Him, who have been called according to His purpose.

2 Corinthians 1

3 Praise be to the God and Father of our Lord Jesus Christ, the Father of compassion and the God of all comfort, 4 who comforts us in all our troubles, so that we can comfort those in any trouble with the comfort we ourselves have received from God. 5 For just as the sufferings of Christ flow over into our lives, so also through Christ our comfort overflows.

2 Corinthians 4

17 For our light and momentary troubles are achieving for us an eternal glory that far outweighs them all. 18 So we fix our eyes not on what is seen, but on what is unseen. For what is seen is temporary, but what is unseen is eternal.

2 Corinthians 12

9 "My grace is sufficient for you, for my power is made perfect in weakness." Therefore I will boast all the more gladly about my weaknesses, so that Christ's power may rest on me. 10 That is why, for Christ's sake, I delight in weaknesses, in insults, in hardships, in persecutions, in difficulties. For when I am weak, then I am strong.

Ephesians 6

10 Finally, be strong in the Lord and in His mighty power. 11 Put on the full armor of God so that you can take your stand against the devil's schemes. 12 For our struggle is not against flesh and blood, but against the rulers, against the authorities, against the powers of this dark world and against the spiritual forces of evil in the heavenly realms.

James 1

2 Consider it pure joy, my brothers, whenever you face trials of many kinds, 3 because you know that the testing of your faith develops perseverance. 4 Perseverance must finish its work so that you may be mature and complete, not lacking anything.

James 5

11 As you know, we consider blessed those who have persevered. You have heard of Job's perseverance and have seen what the Lord finally brought about. The Lord is full of compassion and mercy.

1 Peter 1

6 In this you greatly rejoice, though now for a little while you may have had to suffer grief in all kinds of trials. 7 These have come so that your faith —of greater worth than gold, which perishes even though refined by fire—may be proved genuine and may result in praise, glory and honor when Jesus Christ is revealed.

Developing a Proper
ATTITUDE
(See also Desires, Greed, Pride)

1 Samuel 16

7 The Lord does not look at the things man looks at. Man looks at the outward appearance, but the Lord looks at the heart.

Psalm 49

16 Do not be overawed when a man grows rich, when the splendor of his house increases; 17 for he will take nothing with him when he dies, his splendor will not descend with him. 18 Though while he lived he counted himself blessed—and men praise you when you prosper— 19 he will join the generation of his fathers, who will never see the light of life. 20 A man who has riches without understanding is like the beasts that perish.

Proverbs 13

7 One man pretends to be rich, yet has nothing; another pretends to be poor, yet has great wealth.

Proverbs 16

2 All a man's ways seem innocent to him, but motives are weighed by the Lord.

Haggai 1

5 Now this is what the Lord Almighty says: "Give careful thought to your ways. 6 You have planted much, but have harvested little. You eat, but never

have enough. You drink, but never have your fill. You put on clothes, but are not warm. You earn wages, only to put them in a purse with holes in it." 7 This is what the Lord Almighty says: "Give careful thought to your ways."

Matthew 18

21 Then Peter came to Jesus and asked, "Lord, how many times shall I forgive my brother when he sins against me? Up to seven times?" 22 Jesus answered, "I tell you, not seven times, but seventy-seven times. 23 Therefore, the kingdom of heaven is like a king who wanted to settle accounts with his servants. 24 As he began the settlement, a man who owed him ten thousand talents was brought to him. 25 Since he was not able to pay, the master ordered that he and his wife and his children and all that he had be sold to repay the debt. 26 The servant fell on his knees before him. 'Be patient with me,' he begged, 'and I will pay back everything.' 27 The servant's master took pity on him, canceled the debt and let him go. 28 But when that servant went out, he found one of his fellow servants who owed him a hundred denarii. He grabbed him and began to choke him. 'Pay back what you owe me!' he demanded. 29 His fellow servant fell to his knees and begged him, 'Be patient with me, and I will pay you back.' 30 But he refused. Instead, he went off and had the man thrown into prison until he could pay the debt. 31 When the other servants saw what had happened, they were greatly distressed and went and told their master everything that had happened. 32 Then the master called the servant in. 'You wicked servant,' he said, 'I canceled all that debt of yours because you begged me to. 33 Shouldn't you have had mercy on your fellow servant just as I had on you?' 34 In anger his master turned him over to the jailers until he should pay back all he owed. 35 This is how My heavenly Father will treat each of you unless you forgive your brother from your heart."

Matthew 19

16 Now a man came up to Jesus and asked, "Teacher, what good thing must I do to get eternal life?" 17 "Why do you ask Me about what is good?" Jesus replied. "There is only One who is good. If you want to enter life, obey the commandments." 18 "Which ones?" the man inquired. Jesus replied, " 'Do not murder, do not commit adultery, do not steal, do not give false testimony, 19 honor your father and mother,' and 'love your neighbor as yourself.' " 20 "All these I have kept," the young man said. "What do I still lack?" 21 Jesus answered, "If you want to be perfect, go sell your possessions and give to the poor, and you will have treasure in heaven. Then come, follow Me." 22 When the young man heard this, he went away sad, because he had great wealth. 23 Then Jesus said to His disciples, "I tell you the truth, it is hard for a rich man to enter the kingdom of heaven. 24 Again I tell you, it is easier for a camel to go through the eye of a needle than for a rich man to enter the kingdom of God" [also found in Mark 10:17–24 and Luke 18:18–25].

Mark 7

20 He went on: "What comes out of a man is what makes him 'unclean:' 21 For from within, out of men's hearts, come evil thoughts, sexual immorality, theft, murder, adultery, 22 greed, malice, deceit, lewdness, envy, slander, arrogance and folly. 23 All these evils come from inside and make a man 'unclean.' "

Mark 12

30 Love the Lord your God with all your heart and with all your soul and with all your mind and with all your strength.

Luke 16

13 "No servant can serve two masters. Either he will hate the one and love the other, or he will be

devoted to the one and despise the other. You cannot serve both God and Money." 14 The Pharisees, who loved money, heard all this and were sneering at Jesus. 15 He said to them, "You are the ones who justify yourselves in the eyes of men, but God knows your hearts. What is highly valued among men is detestable in God's sight" [verse 13 also found in Matthew 6:24].

1 Corinthians 13

3 If I give all I possess to the poor and surrender my body to the flames, but have not love, I gain nothing.

4 Love is patient, love is kind. It does not envy, it does not boast, it is not proud. 5 It is not rude, it is not self-seeking, it is not easily angered, it keeps no record of wrongs. 6 Love does not delight in evil but rejoices with the truth. 7 It always protects, always trusts, always hopes, always perseveres.

Philippians 2

3 Do nothing out of selfish ambition or vain conceit, but in humility consider others better than yourselves. 4 Each of you should look not only to your own interests, but also to the interests of others.

1 Timothy 6

3 If anyone teaches false doctrines and does not agree to the sound instruction of our Lord Jesus Christ and to godly teaching, 4 he is conceited and understands nothing. He has an unhealthy interest in controversies and arguments that result in envy, quarreling, malicious talk, evil suspicions 5 and constant friction between men of corrupt mind, who have been robbed of the truth and who think that godliness is a means to financial gain.

James 2

1 My brothers, as believers in our glorious Lord Jesus Christ, don't show favoritism. 2 Suppose a man comes into your meeting wearing a gold ring

and fine clothes, and a poor man in shabby clothes also comes in. 3 If you show special attention to the man wearing fine clothes and say, "Here's a good seat for you," but say to the poor man, "You stand there," or, "Sit on the floor by my feet," 4 have you not discriminated among yourselves and become judges with evil thoughts? 5 Listen, my dear brothers: Has not God chosen those who are poor in the eyes of the world to be rich in faith and to inherit the kingdom He promised those who love Him? 6 But you have insulted the poor. Is it not the rich who are exploiting you? Are they not the ones who are dragging you into court? 7 Are they not the ones who are slandering the noble name of Him to whom you belong? 8 If you really keep the royal law found in Scripture, "Love your neighbor as yourself," you are doing right. 9 But if you show favoritism, you sin and are convicted by the law as lawbreakers. 10 For whoever keeps the whole law and yet stumbles at just one point is guilty of breaking all of it.

The Wisdom of BUDGETING
(See also Planning)

Proverbs 14

16 A wise man is cautious and avoids danger; a fool plunges ahead with great confidence (TLB).

Proverbs 22

3 A prudent man foresees the difficulties ahead and prepares for them; the simpleton goes blindly on and suffers the consequences (TLB).

Proverbs 23

23 Get the facts at any price, and hold on tightly to all the good sense you can get (TLB).

Proverbs 24

3,4 Any enterprise is built by wise planning, becomes strong through common sense, and profits wonderfully by keeping abreast of the facts (TLB).

Proverbs 27

23 Be sure you know the condition of your flocks, give careful attention to your herds; 24 for riches do not endure forever, and a crown is not secure for all generations.

Luke 14

28 Suppose one of you wants to build a tower. Will he not first sit down and estimate the cost to see if he has enough money to complete it?

29 For if he lays the foundation and is not able to finish it, everyone who sees it will ridicule him, 30 saying, "This fellow began to build and was not able to finish."

Developing Wise
BUSINESS PRACTICES
(See also Labor, Partnerships)

Leviticus 19

13 Do not hold back the wages of a hired man overnight.

35 Do not use dishonest standards when measuring length, weight or quantity. 36 Use honest scales and honest weights.

Deuteronomy 25

13,14,15 In all your transactions you must use accurate scales and honest measurements, so that you will have a long, good life in the land the Lord your God is giving you. 16 All who cheat with unjust weights and measurements are detestable to the Lord your God (TLB).

2 Samuel 23

3 When one rules over men in righteousness, when he rules in the fear of God, 4 he is like the light of morning at sunrise on a cloudless morning, like the brightness after rain that brings the grass from the earth.

Job 31

13 If I have denied justice to my menservants and maidservants [employees] when they had a grievance against me, 14 what will I do when God confronts me? What will I answer when called to account?

Proverbs 3

27 Do not withhold good from those who deserve it, when it is in your power to act.

Proverbs 11

26 People curse the man who hoards grain, but blessing crowns him who is willing to sell.

Proverbs 16

11 The Lord demands fairness in every business deal. He established this principle (TLB).

Proverbs 20

14 "It's no good, it's no good!" says the buyer; then off he goes and boasts about his purchase.

Proverbs 24

3,4 Any enterprise is built by wise planning, becomes strong through common sense, and profits wonderfully by keeping abreast of the facts (TLB).

27 Develop your business first before building your house (TLB).

Proverbs 26

10 Like an archer who wounds at random is he who hires a fool or any passer-by.

Proverbs 28

2 A man of understanding and knowledge maintains order.

16 A tyrannical ruler lacks judgment, but he who hates ill-gotten gain will enjoy a long life.

Isaiah 58

6 You stop oppressing those who work for you and treat them fairly and give them what they earn (TLB).

Ezekiel 45

10 You must use honest scales, honest bushels, honest gallons (TLB).

Micah 6

11 Shall I acquit a man with dishonest scales, with a bag of false weights?

Matthew 10

10 For the worker is worth his keep.

Romans 4

4 Now when a man works, his wages are not credited to him as a gift, but as an obligation.

Colossians 4

1 Masters [employers], provide your slaves [employees] with what is right and fair, because you know that you also have a Master in heaven.

1 Timothy 5

18 For the Scripture says, "Do not muzzle the ox while it is treading out the grain," and "The worker deserves his wages" [also found in Luke 10:7].

CONTENTMENT
in Your Current Situation
(See also Attitude, Desires, Greed)

Psalm 17

15 But as for me, my contentment is not in wealth but in seeing You and knowing all is well between us. And when I awake in heaven, I will be fully satisfied, for I will see You face to face (TLB).

Proverbs 10

22 The blessing of the Lord brings wealth, and He adds no trouble to it.

Proverbs 14

30 A heart at peace gives life to the body, but envy rots the bones.

Proverbs 17

1 Better a dry crust with peace and quiet than a house full of feasting, with strife.

Proverbs 19

23 The fear of the Lord leads to life: then one rests content, untouched by trouble.

Proverbs 30

7 Two things I ask of you, O Lord; do not refuse me before I die: 8 Keep falsehood and lies far from me; give me neither poverty nor riches, but give me only my daily bread. 9 Otherwise, I may have too

much and disown You and say, "Who is the Lord?" Or I may become poor and steal, and so dishonor the name of my God.

Ecclesiastes 4

6 Better one handful with tranquillity than two handfuls with toil and chasing after the wind. 7 Again I saw something meaningless under the sun: 8 There was a man all alone; he had neither son nor brother. There was no end to his toil, yet his eyes were not content with his wealth. "For whom am I toiling," he asked, "and why am I depriving myself of enjoyment?" This too is meaningless—a miserable business!

Ecclesiastes 5

10 Whoever loves money never has money enough; whoever loves wealth is never satisfied with his income. This too is meaningless. 11 As goods increase, so do those who consume them. And what benefit are they to the owner except to feast his eyes on them? 12 The sleep of a laborer is sweet, whether he eats little or much, but the abundance of a rich man permits him no sleep.

19 Moreover, when God gives any man wealth and possessions, and enables him to enjoy them, to accept his lot and be happy in his work—this is a gift of God. 20 He seldom reflects on the days of his life, because God keeps him occupied with gladness of heart.

Ecclesiastes 6

6 Though a man lives a thousand years twice over, but doesn't find contentment—well, what's the use? (TLB).

John 14

27 Peace I leave with you; my peace I give you. I do not give to you as the world gives. Do not let your hearts be troubled and do not be afraid.

Philippians 4

11 I am not saying this because I am in need, for I have learned to be content whatever the circumstances. 12 I know what it is to be in need, and I know what it is to have plenty. I have learned the secret of being content in any and every situation, whether well fed or hungry, whether living in plenty or in want. 13 I can do everything through Him who gives me strength.

1 Thessalonians 5

16 Be joyful always; 17 pray continually; 18 give thanks in all circumstances, for this is God's will for you in Christ Jesus.

1 Timothy 6

3 If anyone teaches false doctrines and does not agree to the sound instruction of our Lord Jesus Christ and to godly teaching, 4 he is conceited and understands nothing. He has an unhealthy interest in controversies and arguments that result in envy, quarreling, malicious talk, evil suspicions 5 and constant friction between men of corrupt mind, who have been robbed of the truth and who think that godliness is a means to financial gain. 6 But godliness with contentment is great gain. 7 For we brought nothing into the world, and we can take nothing out of it. 8 But if we have food and clothing, we will be content with that.

Hebrews 13

5 Keep your lives free from the love of money and be content with what you have, because God has said, "Never will I leave you; never will I forsake you."

God's Perspective on
COSIGNING
(See also Debt)

Proverbs 6

1 My son, if you have put up security for your neighbor, if you have struck hands in pledge for another, 2 if you have been trapped by what you said, ensnared by the words of your mouth, 3 then do this, my son, to free yourself, since you have fallen into your neighbor's hands: Go and humble yourself; press your plea with your neighbor! 4 Allow no sleep to your eyes, no slumber to your eyelids. 5 Free yourself, like a gazelle from the hand of the hunter, like a bird from the snare of the fowler.

Proverbs 11

15 He who puts up security for another will surely suffer, but whoever refuses to strike hands in pledge is safe.

Proverbs 17

18 A man lacking in judgment strikes hands in pledge and puts up security for his neighbor.

Proverbs 20

16 Take the garment of one who puts up security for a stranger; hold it in pledge if he does it for a wayward woman [also found in Proverbs 27:13].

Proverbs 22

26 Do not be a man who strikes hands in pledge or puts up security for debts; 27 if you lack the means to pay, your very bed will be snatched from under you.

The Importance of Wise COUNSEL
(See also Wisdom)

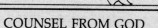

COUNSEL FROM GOD
1 Kings 22

5 First seek the counsel of the Lord.

Psalm 16

7 I will bless the Lord who counsels me; He gives me wisdom in the night. He tells me what to do (TLB).

Psalm 25

12 Who, then, is the man that fears the Lord? He will instruct him in the way chosen for him. 13 He will spend his days in prosperity, and his descendants will inherit the land. 14 The Lord confides in those who fear Him; He makes His covenant known to them.

Psalm 32

8 I (the Lord) will instruct you and teach you in the way you should go; I will counsel you and watch over you. 9 Do not be like the horse or the mule, which have no understanding but must be controlled by bit and bridle or they will not come to you.

Proverbs 1

32 For the waywardness of the simple will kill them, and the complacency of fools will destroy them; 33 but whoever listens to me will live in safety and be at ease, without fear of harm.

Proverbs 2

6 For the Lord gives wisdom, and from His mouth come knowledge and understanding. 7 He holds victory in store for the upright, He is a shield to those whose walk is blameless.

Proverbs 8

8 All the words of my mouth are just; none of them is crooked or perverse. 9 To the discerning all of them are right; they are faultless to those who have knowledge. 10 Choose my instruction instead of silver, knowledge rather than choice gold, 11 for wisdom is more precious than rubies, and nothing you desire can compare with her.

Proverbs 16

20 Whoever gives heed to instruction prospers, and blessed is he who trusts in the Lord.

Proverbs 22

17,18,19 Listen to this wise advice; follow it closely, for it will do you good, and you can pass it on to others: Trust in the Lord (TLB).

Proverbs 29

13 Rich and poor are alike in this: each depends on God for light (TLB).

Isaiah 30

1 Woe to my rebellious children, says the Lord; you ask advice from everyone but Me, and decide to do what I don't want you to do. You yoke yourselves with unbelievers, thus piling up your sins (TLB).

Matthew 4

4 Jesus answered, "It is written: 'Man does not live on bread alone, but on every word that comes from the mouth of God'" [also found in Luke 4:4 and Deuteronomy 8:3b].

Luke 6

46 Why do you call Me, "Lord, Lord," and do not do what I say? 47 I will show you what he is like who comes to Me and hears My words and puts them into practice. 48 He is like a man building a house, who dug down deep and laid the foundation on rock. When a flood came, the torrent struck that house but could not shake it, because it was well built. 49 But the one who hears my words and does not put them into practice is like a man who built a house on the ground without a foundation. The moment the torrent struck that house, it collapsed and its destruction was complete [also found in Matthew 7:24–27].

John 8

47 He who belongs to God hears what God says.

John 10

27 My sheep listen to My voice; I know them and they follow Me.

John 14

16 And I will ask the Father, and He will give you another Counselor to be with you forever— 17 the Spirit of truth. The world cannot accept Him, because it neither sees Him nor knows Him. But you know Him, for He lives with you and will be in you.

26 But the Counselor, the Holy Spirit, whom the Father will send in My name, will teach you all things and will remind you of everything I have said to you.

1 Corinthians 2

14 The man without the Spirit does not accept the things that come from the Spirit of God, for they are foolishness to him, and he cannot understand them, because they are spiritually discerned. 15 The spiritual man makes judgments about all things, but he himself is not subject to any man's judgment: 16 "For who has known the mind of the

Lord that he may instruct Him?" But we have the mind of Christ.

COUNSEL FROM GOD'S WORD
Joshua 1

8 Do not let this book of the law depart from your mouth; meditate on it day and night, so that you may be careful to do everything written in it. Then you will be prosperous and successful.

1 Kings 2

3 Observe what the Lord your God requires: Walk in His ways, and keep His decrees and commands, His laws and requirements, as written in the Law of Moses, so that you may prosper in all you do and wherever you go.

Psalm 1

1 Blessed is the man who does not walk in the counsel of the wicked or stand in the way of sinners or sit in the seat of mockers. 2 But his delight is in the law of the Lord, and on His law he meditates day and night. 3 He is like a tree planted by streams of water, which yields its fruit in season and whose leaf does not wither. Whatever he does prospers.

Psalm 19

7 The law of the Lord is perfect, reviving the soul. The statutes of the Lord are trustworthy, making wise the simple. 8 The precepts of the Lord are right, giving joy to the heart. The commands of the Lord are radiant, giving light to the eyes. 9 The fear of the Lord is pure, enduring forever. The ordinances of the Lord are sure and altogether righteous. 10 They are more precious than gold, than much pure gold; they are sweeter than honey, than honey from the comb.

Psalm 119

9 How can a young man keep his way pure? By living according to Your word. 10 I seek You with all my heart; do not let me stray from Your com-

mands. 11 I have hidden Your word in my heart that I might not sin against You. 12 Praise be to You, O Lord; teach me Your decrees. 13 With my lips I recount all the laws that come from Your mouth. 14 I rejoice in following Your statutes as one rejoices in great riches. 15 I meditate on Your precepts and consider Your ways. 16 I delight in Your decrees; I will not neglect Your word.

24 Your statutes are my delight; they are my counselors.

96 Nothing is perfect except Your words. 97 Oh, how I love them. I think about them all day long. 98 They make me wiser than my enemies, because they are my constant guide. 99 Yes, wiser than my teachers, for I am ever thinking of Your rules. 100 They make me even wiser than the aged. 101 I have refused to walk the paths of evil for I will remain obedient to Your word. 102,103 No, I haven't turned away from what You taught me; Your words are sweeter than honey. 104 And since only Your rules can give me wisdom and understanding, no wonder I hate every false teaching (TLB).

105 Your word is a lamp to my feet and a light for my path.

162 I rejoice in Your laws like one who finds a great treasure (TLB).

Proverbs 3
1 My son, do not forget my teaching, but keep my commands in your heart, 2 for they will prolong your life many years and bring you prosperity. 3 Let love and faithfulness never leave you; bind them around your neck, write them on the tablet of your heart. 4 Then you will win favor and a good name in the sight of God and man.

Proverbs 30
5 Every word of God is flawless; He is a shield to those who take refuge in Him.

Isaiah 55

10 As the rain and the snow come down from heaven, and do not return to it without watering the earth and making it bud and flourish, so that it yields seed for the sower and bread for the eater, 11 so is My word that goes out from My mouth: It will not return to me empty, but will accomplish what I desire and achieve the purpose for which I sent it.

Mark 4

18 Still others, like seed sown among thorns, hear the word; 19 but the worries of this life, the deceitfulness of wealth and the desires for other things come in and choke the word, making it unfruitful. 20 Others, like seed sown on good soil, hear the word, accept it, and produce a crop—thirty, sixty or even a hundred times what was sown [also found in Matthew 13:22 and Luke 8:14].

Romans 15

4 For everything that was written in the past was written to teach us, so that through endurance and the encouragement of the Scriptures we might have hope.

Colossians 3

16 Let the word of Christ dwell in you richly as you teach and admonish one another with all wisdom, and as you sing psalms, hymns and spiritual songs with gratitude in your hearts to God.

1 Thessalonians 2

13 And we also thank God continually because, when you received the word of God, which you heard from us, you accepted it not as the word of men, but as it actually is, the word of God, which is at work in you who believe.

2 Timothy 2

15 Do your best to present yourself to God as one approved, a workman who does not need to be

ashamed and who correctly handles the word of truth.

2 Timothy 3

16 All Scripture is God-breathed and is useful for teaching, rebuking, correcting and training in righteousness, so that the man of God may be thoroughly equipped for every good work.

Hebrews 4

12 The word of God is living and active. Sharper than any double-edged sword, it penetrates even to dividing soul and spirit, joints and marrow; it judges the thoughts and attitudes of the heart.

James 1

22 Do not merely listen to the word, and so deceive yourselves. Do what it says. 23 Anyone who listens to the word but does not do what it says is like a man who looks at his face in a mirror 24 and, after looking at himself, goes away and immediately forgets what he looks like. 25 But the man who looks intently into the perfect law that gives freedom, and continues to do this, not forgetting what he has heard, but doing it—he will be blessed in what he does.

COUNSEL FROM OTHERS
Job 21

16 But their prosperity is not in their own hands, so I stand aloof from the counsel of the wicked.

Psalm 1

1 Blessed is the man who does not walk in the counsel of the wicked or stand in the way of sinners or sit in the seat of mockers. 2 But his delight is in the law of the Lord, and on his law he meditates day and night. 3 He is like a tree planted by streams of water, which yields its fruit in season and whose leaf does not wither. Whatever he does prospers.

Psalm 37

30,31 The godly man is a good counselor because he is just and fair and knows right from wrong (TLB).

Proverbs 1

5 A wise man will hear, and will increase learning; and a man of understanding shall attain unto wise counsel (KJV).

Proverbs 12

15 The way of a fool seems right to him, but a wise man listens to advice.

26 The good man asks advice from friends; the wicked plunge ahead—and fall (TLB).

Proverbs 13

14 The advice of a wise man refreshes like water from a mountain spring. Those accepting it become aware of the pitfalls on ahead (TLB).

20 He who walks with the wise grows wise, but a companion of fools suffers harm.

Proverbs 14

7 If you are looking for advice, stay away from fools (TLB).

Proverbs 15

22 Plans fail for lack of counsel, but with many advisers they succeed.

Proverbs 19

20 Listen to advice and accept instruction and in the end you will be wise.

Proverbs 20

18 Make plans by seeking advice.

Proverbs 21

11 The wise man learns by listening (TLB).

Proverbs 24

6 There is safety in many counselors (TLB).

Proverbs 27

17 As irons sharpens iron, so one man sharpens another.

Ecclesiastes 9

17 The quiet words of the wise are more to be heeded than the shouts of a ruler of fools.

COUNSEL TO OTHERS
Proverbs 10

13 Men with common sense are admired as counselors (TLB).

21 A godly man gives good advice, but a rebel is destroyed by lack of common sense (TLB).

31 The good man gives wise advice, but the liar's counsel is shunned (TLB).

Proverbs 12

18 Reckless words pierce like a sword, but the tongue of the wise brings healing.

Proverbs 15

4 The tongue that brings healing is a tree of life, but a deceitful tongue crushes the spirit.

7 The lips of the wise spread knowledge; not so the hearts of fools.

23 Everyone enjoys giving good advice, and how wonderful it is to be able to say the right thing at the right time! (TLB).

Proverbs 16

21 The wise in heart are called discerning, and pleasant words promote instruction.

23 A wise man's heart guides his mouth, and his lips promote instruction.

Proverbs 24

7 Wisdom is too much for a rebel. He'll not be chosen as a counselor! (TLB).

Proverbs 25

11 Timely advice is as lovely as golden apples in a silver basket (TLB).

12 Like an earring of gold or an ornament of fine gold is a wise man's rebuke to a listening ear.

Proverbs 28

23 He who rebukes a man will in the end gain more favor than he who has a flattering tongue.

Ephesians 4

29 Do not let any unwholesome talk come out of your mouths, but only what is helpful for building others up according to their needs, that it may benefit those who listen.

1 Thessalonians 5

11 Therefore encourage one another and build each other up.

COUNSEL FOR HUSBAND AND WIFE

Genesis 2

18 The Lord God said, "It is not good for the man to be alone. I will make a helper suitable for him."

23 The man said, "This is now bone of my bones and flesh of my flesh; she shall be called 'woman,' for she was taken out of man." 24 For this reason a man will leave his father and mother and be united to his wife, and they will become one flesh.

Proverbs 12

4 A worthy wife is her husband's joy and crown; the other kind corrodes his strength and tears down everything he does (TLB).

Proverbs 14

1 The wise woman builds her house, but with her own hands the foolish one tears hers down.

Proverbs 19

14 Houses and wealth are inherited from parents, but a prudent wife is from the Lord.

Proverbs 31

10 If you can find a truly good wife, she is worth more than precious gems! 11 Her husband can trust her, and she will richly satisfy his needs. 12 She will not hinder him, but help him all her life (TLB).

26 She [a wife of noble character] speaks with wisdom, and faithful instruction is on her tongue. 27 She watches over the affairs of her household and does not eat the bread of idleness. 28 Her children arise and call her blessed; her husband also, and he praises her: 29 "Many women do noble things, but you surpass them all." 30 Charm is deceptive, and beauty is fleeting; but a woman who fears the Lord is to be praised. 31 Give her the reward she has earned, and let her works bring her praise at the city gate.

Malachi 2

13 Another thing you do: You flood the Lord's altar with tears. You weep and wail because He no longer pays attention to your offerings or accepts them with pleasure from your hands. 14 You ask, "Why?" It is because the Lord is acting as the witness between you and the wife of your youth, because you have broken faith with her, though she is your partner, the wife of your marriage covenant. 15 Has not the Lord made them one? In flesh and spirit they are His. And why one? Because He was seeking godly offspring. So guard yourself in your spirit, and do not break faith with the wife of your youth.

Ephesians 5

21 Submit to one another out of reverence for Christ. 22 Wives, submit to your husbands as to the Lord. 23 For the husband is the head of the wife as Christ is the head of the church, His body, of which He is the Savior. 24 Now as the church submits to Christ, so also wives should submit to their husbands in everything. 25 Husbands, love your wives, just as Christ loved the church and gave Himself up for her.

28 In this same way, husbands ought to love their wives as their own bodies. He who loves his wife loves himself. 29 After all, no one ever hated his own body, but he feeds and cares for it, just as Christ does the church— 30 for we are members of his body. 31 "For this reason a man will leave his father and mother and be united to his wife, and the two will become one flesh." 32 This is a profound mystery—but I am talking about Christ and the church. 33 However, each one of you also must love his wife as he loves himself, and the wife must respect her husband.

Colossians 3

18 Wives, submit to your husbands, as it is fitting in the Lord. 19 Husbands, love your wives and do not be harsh with them.

1 Peter 3

7 Husbands, in the same way be considerate as you live with your wives, and treat them with respect as the weaker partner and as heirs with you of the gracious gift of life, so that nothing will hinder your prayers.

COUNSEL FOR CHILDREN
Proverbs 13

1 A wise son heeds his father's instruction, but a mocker does not listen to rebuke.

Proverbs 15

5 A fool spurns his father's discipline, but whoever heeds correction shows prudence.

Proverbs 19

27 Stop listening to instruction, my son, and you will stray from the words of knowledge.

Proverbs 28

24 He who robs his father or mother and says, "It's not wrong"—he is partner to him who destroys.

Proverbs 29

3 A man who loves wisdom brings joy to his father.

Ecclesiastes 12

1 Remember your Creator in the days of your youth, before the days of trouble come and the years approach when you will say, "I find no pleasure in them".

1 Timothy 4

12 Don't let anyone look down on you because you are young, but set an example for the believers in speech, in life, in love, in faith and in purity.

God's Perspective on
DEBT
(See also Cosigning, Lending)

Psalm 7

15 He who digs a hole and scoops it out falls into the pit he has made.

Psalm 37

21 The wicked borrow and do not repay, but the righteous give generously.

Proverbs 3

27 Do not withhold good from those who deserve it, when it is in your power to act. 28 Do not say to your neighbor, "Come back later; I'll give it tomorrow"—when you now have it with you.

Proverbs 11

29 He who brings trouble on his family will inherit only wind, and the fool will be servant to the wise.

Proverbs 22

7 The rich rule over the poor, and the borrower is servant to the lender.

26 Do not be a man who strikes hands in pledge or puts up security for debts; 27 if you lack the means to pay, your very bed will be snatched from under you.

Proverbs 27

12 The prudent see danger and take refuge, but the simple keep going and suffer for it.

Matthew 6

12 Forgive us our debts, as we also have forgiven our debtors.

Romans 13

7 Give everyone what you owe him: If you owe taxes, pay taxes; if revenue, then revenue; if respect, then respect; if honor, then honor. 8 Let no debt remain outstanding, except the continuing debt to love one another, for he who loves his fellow man has fulfilled the law.

Dealing With
DESIRES
(See also Attitude, Greed)

Psalm 37

4 Delight yourself in the Lord and He will give you the desires of your heart.

Psalm 145

13 The Lord is faithful to all His promises and loving toward all He has made. 14 The Lord upholds all those who fall and lifts up all who are bowed down. 15 The eyes of all look to You, and You give them their food at the proper time. 16 You open Your hand and satisfy the desires of every living thing.

Proverbs 12

12 The wicked desire the plunder of evil men, but the root of the righteous flourishes. 13 An evil man is trapped by his sinful talk, but a righteous man escapes trouble.

Proverbs 13

4 The sluggard craves and gets nothing, but the desires of the diligent are fully satisfied.

Proverbs 21

2 All a man's ways seem right to him, but the Lord weighs the heart.

Matthew 7

7 Ask and it will be given to you; seek and you will find; knock and the door will be opened to you.

8 For everyone who asks receives; he who seeks finds; and to him who knocks, the door will be opened. 9 Which of you, if his son asks for bread, will give him a stone? 10 Or if he asks for a fish, will give him a snake? 11 If you, then, though you are evil, know how to give good gifts to your children, how much more will your Father in heaven give good gifts to those who ask Him! [also found in Luke 11:9–13].

John 16

23 I tell you the truth, My Father will give you whatever you ask in My name. 24 Until now you have not asked for anything in My name. Ask and you will receive, and your joy will be complete.

Romans 13

14 Clothe yourselves with the Lord Jesus Christ, and do not think about how to gratify the desires of the sinful nature.

Galatians 5

16 So I say, live by the Spirit, and you will not gratify the desires of the sinful nature. 17 For the sinful nature desires what is contrary to the Spirit, and the Spirit what is contrary to the sinful nature. They are in conflict with each other, so that you do not do what you want.

Galatians 6

7 Do not be deceived: God cannot be mocked. A man reaps what he sows. 8 The one who sows to please his sinful nature, from that nature will reap destruction; the one who sows to please the Spirit, from the Spirit will reap eternal life.

Ephesians 4

22 You were taught, with regard to your former way of life, to put off your old self, which is being corrupted by its deceitful desires; 23 to be made new in the attitude of your minds; 24 and to put on

the new self, created to be like God in true righteousness and holiness.

Colossians 3

1 Since, then, you have been raised with Christ, set your hearts on things above, where Christ is seated at the right hand of God. 2 Set your minds on things above, not on earthly things.

5 Put to death, therefore, whatever belongs to your earthly nature: sexual immorality, impurity, lust, evil desires and greed, which is idolatry.

1 Timothy 6

9 People who want to get rich fall into temptation and a trap and into many foolish and harmful desires that plunge men into ruin and destruction. 10 For the love of money is a root of all kinds of evil. Some people, eager for money, have wandered from the faith and pierced themselves with many griefs. 11 But you, man of God, flee from all this, and pursue righteousness, godliness, faith, love, endurance and gentleness.

James 1

13 When tempted, no one should say, "God is tempting me." For God cannot be tempted by evil, nor does He tempt anyone; 14 but each one is tempted when, by his own evil desire, he is dragged away and enticed. 15 Then, after desire has conceived, it gives birth to sin; and sin, when it is full-grown, gives birth to death. 16 Don't be deceived, my dear brothers.

James 4

1 What causes fights and quarrels among you? Don't they come from your desires that battle within you? 2 You want something but don't get it. You kill and covet, but you cannot have what you want. You quarrel and fight. You do not have, because you do not ask God. 3 When you ask, you do not re-

ceive, because you ask with wrong motives, that you may spend what you get on your pleasures.

1 Peter 1

14 As obedient children, do not conform to the evil desires you had when you lived in ignorance.

2 Peter 2

19 For a man is a slave to whatever has mastered him. 20 If they have escaped the corruption of the world by knowing our Lord and Savior Jesus Christ and are again entangled in it and overcome, they are worse off at the end than they were at the beginning.

1 John 2

15 Do not love the world or anything in the world. If anyone loves the world, the love of the Father is not in him. 16 For everything in the world—the cravings of sinful man, the lust of his eyes and the boastings of what he has and does—comes not from the Father but from the world. 17 The world and its desires pass away, but the man who does the will of God lives forever.

Wisdom in
GIVING
(See also Sharing)

Exodus 22

29 Do not hold back offerings from your granaries or your vats.

Exodus 23

19 Bring the best of the firstfruits of your soil to the house of the Lord your God [also found in Exodus 34:26].

Leviticus 27

30 A tithe of everything from the land, whether grain from the soil or fruit from the trees, belongs to the Lord; it is holy to the Lord.

Deuteronomy 14

22 Be sure to set aside a tenth of all that your fields produce each year.

23 The purpose of tithing is to teach you always to put God first in your lives (TLB).

Deuteronomy 16

16 No man should appear before the Lord empty-handed; 17 Each of you must bring a gift in proportion to the way the Lord your God has blessed you.

Proverbs 3

9 Honor the Lord with your wealth, with the first-fruits of all your crops; 10 then your barns will be

filled to overflowing, and your vats will brim over with new wine.

Proverbs 11

24 One man gives freely, yet gains even more; another withholds unduly, but comes to poverty. 25 A generous man will prosper; he who refreshes others will himself be refreshed.

Ecclesiastes 11

1 Give generously, for your gifts will return to you later. 2 Divide your gifts among many, for in the days ahead you yourself may need much help (TLB).

Malachi 3

8 "Will a man rob God? Yet you rob Me. But you ask, 'How do we rob You?' In tithes and offerings. 9 You are under a curse—the whole nation of you—because you are robbing Me. 10 Bring the whole tithe into the storehouse, that there may be food in My house. Test Me in this," says the Lord Almighty, "and see if I will not throw open the floodgates of heaven and pour out so much blessing that you will not have room enough for it. 11 I will prevent pests from devouring your crops, and the vines in your fields will not cast their fruit," says the Lord Almighty.

Matthew 5

23 Therefore, if you are offering your gift at the altar and there remember that your brother has something against you, 24 leave your gift there in front of the altar. First go and be reconciled to your brother; then come and offer your gift.

Matthew 10

8 Freely you have received, freely give.

Matthew 23

23 Woe to you, teachers of the law and Pharisees, you hypocrites! You give a tenth of your spices—mint, dill and cummin. But you have neglected the

more important matters of the law—justice, mercy and faithfulness. You should have practiced the latter, without neglecting the former [also found in Luke 11:42].

Mark 4

24 "Consider carefully what you hear," He continued. "With the measure you use, it will be measured to you—and even more. 25 Whoever has will be given more; whoever does not have, even what he has will be taken from him."

Mark 12

41 Jesus sat down opposite the place where the offerings were put and watched the crowd putting their money into the temple treasury. Many rich people threw in large amounts. 42 But a poor widow came and put in two very small copper coins, worth only a fraction of a penny. 43 Calling His disciples to him, Jesus said, "I tell you the truth, this poor widow has put more into the treasury than all the others. 44 They all gave out of their wealth; but she, out of her poverty, put in everything—all she had to live on" [also found in Luke 21:1–4].

Luke 6

30 Give to everyone who asks you, and if anyone takes what belongs to you, do not demand it back. 31 Do to others as you would have them do to you. 32 If you love those who love you, what credit is that to you? Even "sinners" love those who love them. 33 And if you do good to those who are good to you, what credit is that to you? Even "sinners" do that.

38 Give, and it will be given to you. A good measure, pressed down, shaken together and running over, will be poured into your lap. For with the measure you use, it will be measured to you.

1 Corinthians 16

2 On every Lord's Day each of you should put aside something from what you have earned during

the week, and use it for this offering. The amount depends on how much the Lord has helped you earn (TLB).

2 Corinthians 9

6 Remember this: Whoever sows sparingly will also reap sparingly, and whoever sows generously will also reap generously.

7 Each man should give what he has decided in his heart to give, not reluctantly or under compulsion, for God loves a cheerful giver. 8 And God is able to make all grace abound to you, so that in all things at all times, having all that you need, you will abound in every good work. 9 As it is written: "He has scattered abroad His gifts to the poor; His righteousness endures forever." 10 Now He who supplies seed to the sower and bread for food will also supply and increase your store of seed and will enlarge the harvest of your righteousness. 11 You will be made rich in every way so that you can be generous on every occasion, and through us your generosity will result in thanksgiving to God. 12 This service that you perform is not only supplying the needs of God's people but is also overflowing in many expressions of thanks to God. 13 Because of the service by which you have proved yourselves, men will praise God for the obedience that accompanies your confession of the gospel of Christ, and for your generosity in sharing with them and with everyone else. 14 And in their prayers for you their hearts will go out to you, because of the surpassing grace God has given you. 15 Thanks be to God for His indescribable gift!

How to Handle
GREED
(see also Attitude, Desires)

Exodus 20

17 You shall not covet your neighbor's house. You shall not covet your neighbor's wife, or his manservant or maidservant, his ox or donkey, or anything that belongs to your neighbor [also found in Deuteronomy 5:21].

Proverbs 15

27 A greedy man brings trouble to his family, but he who hates bribes will live.

Proverbs 24

19,20 Don't envy the wicked. Don't covet his riches. For the evil man has no future; his light will be snuffed out (TLB).

Proverbs 25

27 It is not good to eat too much honey nor is it honorable to seek one's own honor. 28 Like a city whose walls are broken down is a man who lacks self-control.

Proverbs 28

20 The man who wants to do right will get a rich reward. But the man who wants to get rich quick will quickly fail (TLB).

22 A stingy man is eager to get rich and is unaware that poverty awaits him.

25 A greedy man stirs up dissension, but he who trusts in the Lord will prosper.

Matthew 6

19 Do not store up for yourselves treasures on earth, where moth and rust destroy, and where thieves break in and steal. 20 But store up for yourselves treasures in heaven, where moth and rust do not destroy, and where thieves do not break in and steal. 21 For where your treasure is, there your heart will be also [also found in Luke 12:33,34].

Luke 12

15 Then He [Jesus] said to them, "Watch out! Be on your guard against all kinds of greed; a man's life does not consist in the abundance of his possessions." 16 And He told them this parable: "The ground of a certain rich man produced a good crop. 17 He thought to himself, 'What shall I do? I have no place to store my crops.' 18 Then he said, 'This is what I'll do. I will tear down my barns and build bigger ones, and there I will store all my grain and my goods. 19 And I'll say to myself, "You have plenty of good things laid up for many years. Take life easy; eat, drink and be merry." 20 But God said to him, 'You fool! This very night your life will be demanded from you. Then who will get what you have prepared for yourself?' 21 This is how it will be with anyone who stores up things for himself but is not rich toward God."

1 Corinthians 5

11 But now I am writing you that you must not associate with anyone who calls himself a brother but is sexually immoral or greedy, an idolater or a slanderer, a drunkard or a swindler. With such a man do not even eat.

1 Timothy 6

9 People who want to get rich fall into temptation and a trap and into many foolish and harmful desires that plunge men into ruin and destruction.

10 For the love of money is a root of all kinds of evil. Some people, eager for money, have wandered from the faith and pierced themselves with many griefs. 11 But you, man of God, flee from all this, and pursue righteousness, godliness, faith, love, endurance and gentleness.

2 Timothy 3

1 But mark this: There will be terrible times in the last days. 2 People will be lovers of themselves, lovers of money, boastful, proud, abusive, disobedient to their parents, ungrateful, unholy, 3 without love, unforgiving, slanderous, without self-control, brutal, not lovers of the good, 4 treacherous, rash, conceited, lovers of pleasure rather than lovers of God— 5 having a form of godliness but denying its power. Have nothing to do with them.

The Wisdom of
HONESTY
(See also Righteousness)

Leviticus 19

11 Do not steal. Do not lie. Do not deceive one another.

Numbers 30

2 When a man makes a vow to the Lord or takes an oath to obligate himself by a pledge, he must not break his word but must do everything he said.

1 Chronicles 29

17 I know, my God, that You test the heart and are pleased with integrity.

Psalm 62

10 Do not trust in extortion or take pride in stolen goods; though your riches increase, do not set your heart on them.

Proverbs 5

21 For a man's ways are in full view of the Lord, and He examines all his paths.

Proverbs 13

11 Dishonest money dwindles away, but he who gathers money little by little makes it grow.

Proverbs 16

30 He who winks with his eye is plotting perversity; he who purses his lips is bent on evil.

Proverbs 22

16 He who gains by oppressing the poor or by bribing the rich shall end in poverty (TLB).

Proverbs 30

7 Two things I ask of You, O Lord; do not refuse me before I die: 8 Keep falsehood and lies far from me; give me neither poverty nor riches, but give me only my daily bread. 9 Otherwise, I may have too much and disown You and say, 'Who is the Lord?' Or I may become poor and steal, and so dishonor the name of my God.

Ecclesiastes 8

11 Because God does not punish sinners instantly, people feel it is safe to do wrong (TLB).

Jeremiah 17

11 Like a partridge that hatches eggs it did not lay is the man who gains riches by unjust means. When his life is half gone, they will desert him, and in the end he will prove to be a fool.

Matthew 5

37 Simply let your 'Yes' be 'Yes,' and your 'No,' 'No'; anything beyond this comes from the evil one.

Matthew 7

12 In everything, do to others what you would have them do to you, for this sums up the Law and the Prophets [also found in Luke 6:31].

Luke 16

10 Whoever can be trusted with very little can also be trusted with much, and whoever is dishonest with very little will also be dishonest with much. 11 So if you have not been trustworthy in handling worldly wealth, who will trust you with true riches? 12 And if you have not been trustworthy with someone else's property, who will give you property of your own?

Romans 13

9 The commandments, "Do not commit adultery," "Do not murder," "Do not steal," "Do not covet," and whatever other commandment there may be, are summed up in this one rule: "Love your neighbor as yourself." 10 Love does no harm to its neighbor. Therefore love is the fulfillment of the law.

2 Corinthians 13

8 For we cannot do anything against the truth, but only for the truth.

Ephesians 4

28 He who has been stealing must steal no longer, but must work, doing something useful with his own hands, that he may have something to share with those in need.

God's Perspective on
INHERITANCE

Psalm 16

5 The Lord himself is my inheritance, my prize. He is my food and drink, my highest joy! He guards all that is mine. 6 He sees that I am given pleasant brooks and meadows as my share! What a wonderful inheritance! (TLB).

Psalm 37

18 The days of the blameless are known to the Lord, and their inheritance will endure forever. 19 In times of disaster they will not wither; in days of famine they will enjoy plenty.

Psalm 39

4 Show me, O Lord, my life's end and the number of my days; let me know how fleeting is my life. 5 You have made my days a mere handbreadth; the span of my years is as nothing before You. Each man's life is but a breath. 6 Man is a mere phantom as he goes to and fro: He bustles about, but only in vain; he heaps up wealth, not knowing who will get it. 7 But now, Lord, what do I look for? My hope is in You.

Psalm 112

1 Praise the Lord. Blessed is the man who fears the Lord, who finds great delight in His commands. 2 His children will be mighty in the land; each generation of the upright will be blessed. 3 Wealth and riches are in His house, and His righteousness endures forever. 4 Even in darkness light dawns for

the upright, for the gracious and compassionate and righteous man.

Proverbs 11

18 The evil man gets rich for the moment, but the good man's reward lasts forever (TLB).

Proverbs 13

22 A good man leaves an inheritance for his children's children, but a sinner's wealth is stored up for the righteous.

Proverbs 20

21 An inheritance quickly gained at the beginning will not be blessed at the end.

Matthew 5

5 Blessed are the meek, for they will inherit the earth.

10 Blessed are those who are persecuted because of righteousness, for theirs is the kingdom of heaven.

Mark 10

29 "I tell you the truth," Jesus replied, "no one who has left home or brothers or sisters or mother or father or children or fields for Me and the gospel 30 will fail to receive a hundred times as much in this present age (homes, brothers, sisters, mothers, children and fields—and with them, persecutions) and in the age to come, eternal life" [also found in Matthew 19:28,29 and Luke 18:29,30].

1 Corinthians 2

9 As it is written: "No eye has seen, no ear has heard, no mind has conceived what God has prepared for those who love Him."

1 Corinthians 6

9 Do you not know that the wicked will not inherit the kingdom of God? Do not be deceived: Neither

the sexually immoral nor idolaters nor adulterers nor male prostitutes nor homosexual offenders 10 nor thieves nor the greedy nor drunkards nor slanderers nor swindlers will inherit the kingdom of God.

1 Corinthians 15

50 I declare to you, brothers, that flesh and blood cannot inherit the kingdom of God, nor does the perishable inherit the imperishable.

1 Peter 1

3 Praise be to the God and Father of our Lord Jesus Christ! In His great mercy He has given us new birth into a living hope through the resurrection of Jesus Christ from the dead, 4 and into an inheritance that can never perish, spoil or fade—kept in heaven for you.

Revelation 22

12 Behold, I am coming soon! My reward is with Me, and I will give to everyone according to what he has done.

INVESTING
With Wisdom
(See also Money, Savings, Treasure, Wealth)

Proverbs 13

11 Dishonest money dwindles away, but he who gathers money little by little makes it grow.

Proverbs 16

20 Whoever gives heed to instruction prospers, and blessed is he who trusts in the Lord.

Proverbs 21

5 The plans of the diligent lead to profit as surely as haste leads to poverty.

5 Steady plodding brings prosperity; hasty speculation brings poverty. 6 Dishonest gain will never last, so why take the risk? (TLB).

Proverbs 24

3,4 Any enterprise is built by wise planning, becomes strong through common sense, and profits wonderfully by keeping abreast of the facts (TLB).

Proverbs 28

20 The man who wants to do right will get a rich reward. But the man who wants to get rich quick will quickly fail (TLB).

Ecclesiastes 5

13,14 There is another serious problem I have seen everywhere—savings are put into risky investments that turn sour, and soon there is nothing left to pass on to one's son. 15 The man who speculates is soon back to where he began—with nothing. 16 This, as I said, is a very serious problem, for all his hard work has been for nothing; he has been working for the wind. It is all swept away. 17 All the rest of his life he is under a cloud—gloomy, discouraged, frustrated, and angry (TLB).

Matthew 25

14 Again, it will be like a man going on a journey, who called his servants and entrusted his property to them. 15 To one he gave five talents of money, to another two talents, and to another one talent, each according to his ability. Then he went on his journey. 16 The man who had received the five talents went at once and put his money to work and gained five more. 17 So also, the one with the two talents gained two more. 18 But the man who had received the one talent went off, dug a hole in the ground and hid his master's money. 19 After a long time the master of those servants returned and settled accounts with them. 20 The man who had received the five talents brought the other five. "Master," he said, "you entrusted me with five talents. See, I have gained five more." 21 His master replied, "Well done, good and faithful servant! You have been faithful with a few things; I will put you in charge of many things. Come and share your master's happiness!" 22 The man with the two talents also came. "Master," he said, "you entrusted me with two talents; see, I have gained two more." 23 His master replied, "Well done, good and faithful servant! You have been faithful with a few things; I will put you in charge of many things. Come and share your master's happiness! 24 Then the man who had received the one talent came. "Master," he said, "I knew that you are a hard man, harvesting

where you have not sown and gathering where you have not scattered seed. 25 So I was afraid and went out and hid your talent in the ground. See, here is what belongs to you." 26 His master replied, "You wicked, lazy servant! So you knew that I harvest where I have not sown and gather where I have not scattered seed? 27 Well then, you should have put my money on deposit with the bankers, so that when I returned I would have received it back with interest. 28 Take the talent from him and give it to the one who has the ten talents. 29 For everyone who has will be given more, and he will have an abundance. Whoever does not have, even what he has will be taken from him. 30 And throw that worthless servant outside, into the darkness, where there will be weeping and gnashing of teeth" [also found in Luke 19:12–26].

God's View of
JUSTICE
(See also Honesty, Lawsuits, Righteousness)

Exodus 23

7 Have nothing to do with a false charge and do not put an innocent or honest person to death, for I will not acquit the guilty.

Leviticus 5

1 If a person sins because he does not speak up when he hears a public charge to testify regarding something he has seen or learned about, he will be held responsible.

Leviticus 19

15 Do not pervert justice; do not show partiality to the poor or favoritism to the great, but judge your neighbor fairly.

Deuteronomy 1

17 Do not show partiality in judging; hear both small and great alike. Do not be afraid of any man, for judgment belongs to God.

Deuteronomy 16

19 Do not pervert justice or show partiality. Do not accept a bribe, for a bribe blinds the eyes of the wise and twists the words of the righteous.

Deuteronomy 19

15 One witness is not enough to convict a man accused of any crime or offense he may have committed. A matter must be established by the testimony of two or three witnesses.

Deuteronomy 24

17 Do not deprive the alien or the fatherless of justice, or take the cloak of the widow as a pledge.

Psalm 106

3 Blessed are they who maintain justice, who constantly do what is right.

Proverbs 16

8 Better a little with righteousness than much gain with injustice.

Proverbs 21

3 To do what is right and just is more acceptable to the Lord than sacrifice.

Proverbs 31

8 Speak up for those who cannot speak for themselves, for the rights of all who are destitute. 9 Speak up and judge fairly; defend the rights of the poor and needy.

Isaiah 1

17 Learn to do right! Seek justice, encourage the oppressed. Defend the cause of the fatherless, plead the case of the widow.

Isaiah 56

1 This is what the Lord says: "Maintain justice and do what is right, for My salvation is close at hand and My righteousness will soon be revealed."

Isaiah 61

8 For I, the Lord, love justice; I hate robbery and iniquity.

Zechariah 8

16 "These are the things you are to do: Speak the truth to each other, and render true and sound judgment in your courts; 17 do not plot evil against your neighbor, and do not love to swear falsely. I hate all this," declares the Lord.

Matthew 5

7 Blessed are the merciful, for they will be shown mercy.

Luke 6

37 Do not judge, and you will not be judged. Do not condemn, and you will not be condemned. Forgive, and you will be forgiven.

Your Attitude Toward
LABOR
(See also Attitude, Business Practices, Success)

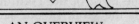

AN OVERVIEW
Genesis 2

15 The Lord God took the man and put him in the Garden of Eden to work it and take care of it.

Genesis 3

17 To Adam He said, "Because you listened to your wife and ate from the tree about which I commanded you, 'You must not eat of it,' cursed is the ground because of you; through painful toil you will eat of it all the days of your life. 18 It will produce thorns and thistles for you, and you will eat the plants of the field. 19 By the sweat of your brow you will eat your food until you return to the ground, since from it you were taken; for dust you are and to dust you will return."

23 So the Lord God banished him [Adam] from the Garden of Eden to work the ground from which he had been taken.

Exodus 20

8 Remember the Sabbath day by keeping it holy. 9 Six days you shall labor and do all your work, 10 but the seventh day is a Sabbath to the Lord your God. On it you shall not do any work, neither you, nor your son or daughter, nor your manservant or maidservant, nor your animals, nor the alien within

your gates. 11 For in six days the Lord made the heavens and the earth, the sea, and all that is in them, but He rested on the seventh day. Therefore the Lord blessed the Sabbath day and made it holy.

Deuteronomy 8

17 You may say to yourself, "My power and the strength of my hands have produced this wealth for me." 18 But remember the Lord your God, for it is He who gives you the ability to produce wealth.

Psalm 90

17 May the favor of the Lord our God rest upon us; establish the work of our hands for us—yes, establish the work of our hands.

Psalm 127

1 Unless the Lord builds the house, its builders labor in vain.

Ecclesiastes 3

12 I know that there is nothing better for men than to be happy and do good while they live. 13 That every man may eat and drink, and find satisfaction in all his toil—this is the gift of God.

Ecclesiastes 5

12 The sleep of a laborer is sweet, whether he eats little or much, but the abundance of a rich man permits him no sleep.
15 Naked a man comes from his mother's womb, and as he comes, so he departs. He takes nothing from his labor that he can carry in his hand. 16 This too is a grievous evil: As a man comes, so he departs, and what does he gain, since he toils for the wind? 17 All his days he eats in darkness, with great frustration, affliction and anger. 18 Then I realized that it is good and proper for a man to eat and drink, and to find satisfaction in his toilsome labor under the sun during the few days of life God has given him—for this is his lot. 19 Moreover, when God gives any man wealth and possessions,

and enables him to enjoy them, to accept his lot and be happy in his work—this is a gift of God. 20 He seldom reflects on the days of his life, because God keeps him occupied with gladness of heart.

John 5

17 Jesus said to them, "My Father is always at His work to this very day, and I, too, am working."

John 6

27 Do not work for food that spoils, but food that endures to eternal life, which the Son of Man will give you. On Him God the Father has placed His seal of approval.

1 Corinthians 9

7 Who serves as a soldier at his own expense? Who plants a vineyard and does not eat of its grapes? Who tends a flock and does not drink of the milk? 8 Do I say this merely from a human point of view? Doesn't the Law say the same thing? 9 For it is written in the Law of Moses: "Do not muzzle an ox while it is treading out the grain." Is it about oxen that God is concerned? 10 Surely He says this for us, doesn't He? Yes, this was written for us, because when the plowman plows and the thresher threshes, they ought to do so in the hope of sharing in the harvest.

Ephesians 6

5 Slaves [employees], obey your earthly masters [employers] with respect and fear, and with sincerity of heart, just as you would obey Christ. 6 Obey them not only to win their favor when their eye is on you, but like slaves of Christ, doing the will of God from your heart. 7 Serve wholeheartedly, as if you were serving the Lord, not men, 8 because you know that the Lord will reward everyone for whatever good he does, whether he is slave or free. 9 And masters [employers], treat your slaves [employees] in the same way. Do not threaten them, since you know that He who is both their

Master and yours is in heaven, and there is no favoritism with Him.

Colossians 3

17 And whatever you do, whether in word or deed, do it all in the name of the Lord Jesus, giving thanks to God the Father through him.

22 Slaves [employees], obey your earthly masters [employers] in everything; and do it, not only when their eye is on you and to win their favor, but with sincerity of heart and reverence for the Lord. 23 Whatever you do, work at it with all your heart, as working for the Lord, not for men. 24 since you know that you will receive an inheritance from the Lord as a reward. It is the Lord Christ you are serving. 25 Anyone who does wrong will be repaid for his wrong, and there is no favoritism.

1 Timothy 5

18 For the Scripture says, "Do not muzzle the ox while it is treading out the grain," and "The worker deserves his wages" [also found in Luke 10:7].

THE DILIGENT WORKER
Proverbs 10

4 Lazy hands make a man poor, but diligent hands bring wealth.

Proverbs 12

11 He who works his land will have abundant food, but he who chases fantasies lacks judgment.

14 From the fruit of his lips a man is filled with good things as surely as the work of his hands rewards him.

24 Diligent hands will rule, but laziness ends in slave labor.

Proverbs 13

4 The sluggard craves and gets nothing, but the desires of the diligent are fully satisfied.

Proverbs 14

23 All hard work brings a profit, but mere talk leads only to poverty.

Proverbs 21

5 The plans of the diligent lead to profit as surely as haste leads to poverty.

Proverbs 22

29 Do you see a man skilled in his work? He will serve before kings; he will not serve before obscure men.

Proverbs 25

13 A faithful employee is as refreshing as a cool day in the hot summertime (TLB).

Proverbs 28

19 He who works his land will have abundant food, but the one who chases fantasies will have his fill of poverty. 20 A faithful man will be richly blessed, but one eager to get rich will not go unpunished.

Ecclesiastes 9

10 Whatever your hand finds to do, do it with all your might.

Ecclesiastes 11

6 Sow your seed in the morning, and at evening let not your hands be idle, for you do not know which will succeed, whether this or that, or whether both will do equally well.

1 Thessalonians 4

11 Make it your ambition to lead a quiet life, to mind your own business and to work with your hands, just as we told you, 12 so that your daily life may win the respect of outsiders and so that you will not be dependent on anybody.

2 Timothy 2

6 The hardworking farmer should be the first to receive a share of the crops.

Titus 3

14 Our people must learn to devote themselves to doing what is good, in order that they may provide for daily necessities and not live unproductive lives.

THE EXCESSIVE WORKER
Psalm 127

2 In vain you rise early and stay up late, toiling for food to eat—for He grants sleep to those He loves.

Proverbs 23

4 Do not wear yourself out to get rich; have the wisdom to show restraint. 5 Cast but a glance at riches, and they are gone, for they will surely sprout wings and fly off to the sky like an eagle.

Ecclesiastes 2

18 I hated all the things I had toiled for under the sun, because I must leave them to the one who comes after me. 19 And who knows whether he will be a wise man or a fool? Yet he will have control over all the work into which I have poured my efforts and skill under the sun. This too is meaningless.

Ecclesiastes 4

7 Again I saw something meaningless under the sun: 8 There was a man all alone; he had neither son nor brother. There was no end to his toil, yet his eyes were not content with his wealth. "For whom am I toiling," he asked, "and why am I depriving myself of enjoyment?" This too is meaningless—a miserable business!

THE LAZY WORKER
Proverbs 6

6 Go to the ant, you sluggard; consider its ways and be wise! 7 It has no commander, no overseer or

ruler, 8 yet it stores its provisions in summer and gathers its food at harvest.

Proverbs 10

26 A lazy fellow is a pain to his employers—like smoke in their eyes or vinegar that sets the teeth on edge (TLB).

Proverbs 12

9 It is better to get your hands dirty—and eat, than to be too proud to work—and starve (TLB).

Proverbs 18

9 One who is slack in his work is brother to one who destroys.

Proverbs 19

15 Laziness brings on deep sleep, and the shiftless man goes hungry.

24 Some men are so lazy they won't even feed themselves! (TLB)

Proverbs 20

4 A sluggard does not plow in season; so at harvest time he looks but finds nothing.

Proverbs 24

30 I went past the field of the sluggard, past the vineyard of the man who lacks judgment; 31 thorns had come up everywhere, the ground was covered with weeds, and the stone wall was in ruins. 32 I applied my heart to what I observed and learned a lesson from what I saw: 33 A little sleep, a little slumber, a little folding of the hands to rest— 34 and poverty will come on you like a bandit and scarcity like an armed man.

Proverbs 26

13 The lazy man won't go out and work. "There might be a lion outside!" he says. 14 He sticks to his bed like a door to its hinges! 15 He is too tired

even to lift his food from his dish to his mouth!
16 Yet in his own opinion he is smarter than seven
wise men (TLB).

Ecclesiastes 4

5 The fool folds his hands and ruins himself.

Ecclesiastes 10

18 If a man is lazy, the rafters sag; if his hands are
idle, the house leaks.

Ecclesiastes 11

4 Whoever watches the wind will not plant; whoever looks at the clouds will not reap.

Romans 12

11 Never be lazy in your work but serve the Lord
enthusiastically (TLB).

2 Thessalonians 3

8 Nor did we eat anyone's food without paying
for it. On the contrary, we worked night and day,
laboring and toiling so that we would not be a burden to any of you. 9 We did this, not because we
do not have the right to such help, but in order to
make ourselves a model for you to follow.
10 For even when we were with you, we gave you
this rule: "If a man will not work, he shall not eat."
11 We hear that some among you are idle. They are
not busy; they are busybodies. 12 Such people we
command and urge in the Lord Jesus Christ, to settle
down and earn the bread they eat.

1 Timothy 5

8 If anyone does not provide for his relatives, and
especially for his immediate family, he has denied
the faith and is worse than an unbeliever.

God's Word Concerning
LAWSUITS
(See also Honesty, Justice, Righteousness)

Exodus 23

1 Do not spread false reports. Do not help a wicked man by being a malicious witness. 2 Do not follow the crowd in doing wrong. When you give testimony in a lawsuit, do not pervert justice by siding with the crowd, 3 and do not show favoritism to a poor man in his lawsuit.

6 Do not deny justice to your poor people in their lawsuits.

Leviticus 19

18 Do not seek revenge or bear a grudge against one of your people, but love your neighbor as yourself. I am the Lord.

Proverbs 3

30 Do not accuse a man for no reason—when he has done you no harm.

Proverbs 20

22 Do not say, "I'll pay you back for this wrong!" Wait for the Lord, and He will deliver you.

Proverbs 24

28 Do not testify against your neighbor without cause, or use your lips to deceive. 29 Do not say,

"I'll do to him as he has done to me; I'll pay that man back for what he did."

Proverbs 25

8,9,10 Don't be hot-headed and rush to court! You may start something you can't finish and go down before your neighbor in shameful defeat. So discuss the matter with him privately. Don't tell anyone else, lest he accuse you of slander and you can't withdraw what you said (TLB).

Matthew 5

40 And if someone wants to sue you and take your tunic, let him have your cloak as well. 41 If someone forces you to go one mile, go with him two miles.

Matthew 7

1 Do not judge, or you too will be judged. 2 For in the same way you judge others, you will be judged, and with the measure you use, it will be measured to you. 3 Why do you look at the speck of sawdust in your brother's eye and pay no attention to the plank in your own eye? 4 How can you say to your brother, "Let me take the speck out of your eye," when all the time there is a plank in your own eye? 5 You hypocrite, first take the plank out of your own eye, and then you will see clearly to remove the speck from your brother's eye [also Luke 6:37 and 41,42].

Matthew 18

15 If your brother sins against you, go and show him his fault, just between the two of you. If he listens to you, you have won your brother over. 16 But if he will not listen, take one or two others along, so that 'every matter may be established by the testimony of two or three witnesses.' 17 If he refuses to listen to them, tell it to the church; and if he refuses to listen even to the church, treat

him as you would a pagan or a tax collector. 18 I tell you the truth, whatever you bind on earth will be bound in heaven and whatever you loose on earth will be loosed in heaven [verse 16 also found in Deuteronomy 19:15; verse 18 also found in Matthew 16:19b].

Romans 12

17 Do not repay anyone evil for evil. Be careful to do what is right in the eyes of everybody. 18 If it is possible, as far as it depends on you, live at peace with everyone. 19 Do not take revenge, my friends, but leave room for God's wrath, for it is written: "It is Mine to avenge; I will repay," says the Lord. 20 On the contrary: "If your enemy is hungry, feed him; if he is thirsty, give him something to drink. In doing this, you will heap burning coals on his head." 21 Do not be overcome by evil, but overcome evil with good [also found in Proverbs 25:21, 22].

1 Corinthians 6

1 If any of you have a dispute with another, dare he take it before the ungodly for judgment instead of before the saints? 2 Do you not know that the saints will judge the world? And if you are to judge the world, are you not competent to judge trivial cases? 3 Do you not know that we will judge angels? How much more the things of this life! 4 Therefore, if you have disputes about such matters, appoint as judges even men of little account in the church! 5 I say this to shame you. Is it possible that there is nobody among you wise enough to judge a dispute between believers? 6 But instead, one brother goes to law against another—and this in front of unbelievers! 7 The very fact that you have lawsuits among you means you have been completely defeated already. Why not rather be wronged? Why not rather be cheated? 8 Instead, you yourselves cheat and do wrong, and you do this to your brothers.

Galatians 5

14 The entire law is summed up in a single command: "Love your neighbor as yourself." 15 If you keep on biting and devouring each other, watch out or you will be destroyed by each other.

Colossians 3

13 Bear with each other and forgive whatever grievances you may have against one another. Forgive as the Lord forgave you.

Hebrews 12

14 Make every effort to live in peace with all men and to be holy; without holiness no one will see the Lord.

LENDING
From a Biblical Perspective
(See also Cosigning, Debt)

Exodus 22

25 If you lend money to one of My people among you who is needy, do not be like a moneylender; charge him no interest. 26 If you take your neighbor's cloak as a pledge, return it to him by sunset, 27 because his cloak is the only covering he has for his body. What else will he sleep in? When he cries out to Me, I will hear, for I am compassionate.

Leviticus 25

35 If one of your countrymen becomes poor and is unable to support himself among you, help him as you would an alien or a temporary resident, so he can continue to live among you. 36 Do not take interest of any kind from him, but fear your God, so that your countryman may continue to live among you. 37 You must not lend him money at interest or sell him food at a profit.

Deuteronomy 15

7 Do not be hardhearted or tightfisted toward your poor brother. 8 Rather be openhanded and freely lend him whatever he needs.

Deuteronomy 23

19 Do not charge your brother interest, whether on money or food or anything else that may earn interest.

Deuteronomy 24

6 Do not take a pair of millstones—not even the upper one—as security for a debt, because that would be taking a man's livelihood as security.

10 When you make a loan of any kind to your neighbor, do not go into his house to get what he is offering as a pledge. 11 Stay outside and let the man to whom you are making the loan bring the pledge out to you. 12 If the man is poor, do not go to sleep with his pledge in your possession. 13 Return his cloak to him by sunset so that he may sleep in it. Then he will thank you, and it will be regarded as a righteous act in the sight of the Lord your God.

Psalm 15

5 . . . who lends his money without usury and does not accept a bribe against the innocent.
He who does these things will never be shaken.

Psalm 37

25 I was young and now I am old, yet I have never seen the righteous forsaken or their children begging bread. 26 They are always generous and lend freely; their children will be blessed.

Psalm 112

5 Good will come to him who is generous and lends freely, who conducts his affairs with justice. 6 Surely he will never be shaken; a righteous man will be remembered forever. 7 He will have no fear of bad news; his heart is steadfast, trusting in the Lord. 8 His heart is secure, he will have no fear; in the end he will look in triumph on his foes. 9 He has scattered abroad his gifts to the poor, his righteousness endures forever; his horn will be lifted high in honor.

Proverbs 28

8 He who increases his wealth by exorbitant interest amasses it for another, who will be kind to the poor.

Ezekiel 18

7 He [a righteous man] does not oppress anyone, but returns what he took in pledge for a loan. He does not commit robbery but gives his food to the hungry and provides clothing for the naked. 8 He does not lend at usury or take excessive interest. He withholds his hand from doing wrong and judges fairly between man and man. 9 He follows my decrees and faithfuly keeps my laws. That man is righteous; he will surely live, declares the Sovereign Lord.

Ezekiel 22

12 You take usury and excessive interest and make unjust gain from your neighbors by extortion. And you have forgotten Me, declares the Sovereign Lord.

Matthew 5

42 Give to the one who asks you, and do not turn away from the one who wants to borrow from you.

Matthew 6

12 Forgive us our debts, as we also have forgiven our debtors.

Matthew 18

21 Then Peter came to Jesus and asked, "Lord, how many times shall I forgive my brother when he sins against me? Up to seven times?" 22 Jesus answered, "I tell you, not seven times, but seventy-seven times [or seventy times seven]. 23 Therefore, the kingdom of heaven is like a king who wanted to settle accounts with his servants. 24 As he began the settlement, a man who owed him ten thousand talents was brought to him. 25 Since he was not able to pay, the master ordered that he and his wife and his children and all that he had be sold to repay the debt. 26 The servant fell on his knees before him. 'Be patient with me,' he begged, 'and I will pay back everything.' 27 The servant's master took pity

on him, canceled the debt and let him go.
28 But when that servant went out, he found one of
his fellow servants who owed him a hundred denarii. He grabbed him and began to choke him. 'Pay
back what you owe me!' he demanded.
29 His fellow servant fell to his knees and begged
him, 'Be patient with me, and I will pay you back.'
30 But he refused. Instead, he went off and had the
man thrown into prison until he could pay the debt.
31 When the other servants saw what had happened, they were greatly distressed and went and
told their master everything that had happened.
32 Then the master called the servant in. 'You
wicked servant,' he said, 'I canceled all that debt of
yours because you begged me to. 33 Shouldn't you
have had mercy on your fellow servant just as I had
on you?' 34 In anger his master turned him over to
the jailers until he should pay back all he owed.
35 This is how My heavenly Father will treat each of
you unless you forgive your brother from your
heart."

Luke 6

34 And if you lend to those from whom you ex-
pect repayment, what credit is that to you? Even
"sinners" lend to "sinners," expecting to be repaid
in full. 35 But love your enemies, do good to them,
and lend to them without expecting to get anything
back. Then your reward will be great, and you will
be sons of the Most High because He is kind to the
ungrateful and wicked. 36 Be merciful, just as your
Father is merciful.

Your Attitude Toward
MONEY
(See also Treasure, Wealth)

Exodus 20

23 Do not make any gods to be alongside Me; do not make for yourselves gods of silver or gods of gold.

Proverbs 17

16 Of what use is money in the hand of a fool, since he has no desire to get wisdom?

Ecclesiastes 5

10 Whoever loves money never has money enough; whoever loves wealth is never satisfied with his income. This too is meaningless. 11 As goods increase, so do those who consume them. And what benefit are they to the owner except to feast his eyes on them? 12 The sleep of a laborer is sweet, whether he eats little or much, but the abundance of a rich man permits him no sleep.

Luke 16

13 "No servant can serve two masters. Either he will hate the one and love the other, or he will be devoted to the one and despise the other. You cannot serve both God and Money." 14 The Pharisees, who loved money, heard all this and were sneering at Jesus. 15 He said to them, "You are the ones who justify yourselves in the eyes of men, but God knows your hearts. What is highly valued among

men is detestable in God's sight" [verse 13 also found in Matthew 6:24].

1 Timothy 6

9 People who want to get rich fall into temptation and a trap and into many foolish and harmful desires that plunge men into ruin and destruction. 10 For the love of money is a root of all kinds of evil. Some people, eager for money, have wandered from the faith and pierced themselves with many griefs. 11 But you, man of God, flee from all this, and pursue righteousness, godliness, faith, love, endurance and gentleness.

Hebrews 13

5 Keep your lives free from the love of money and be content with what you have, because God has said, "Never will I leave you; never will I forsake you."

2 Peter 2

19 For a man is a slave to whatever has mastered him. 20 If they have escaped the corruption of the world by knowing our Lord and Savior Jesus Christ and are again entangled in it and overcome, they are worse off at the end than they were at the beginning.

Meeting Your
NEEDS
(See also Desires)

Genesis 1

29 Then God said, "I give you every seed-bearing plant on the face of the whole earth and every tree that has fruit with seed in it. They will be yours for food. 30 And to all the beasts of the earth and all the birds of the air and all the creatures that move on the ground—everything that has the breath of life in it—I give every green plant for food." And it was so.

Genesis 9

3 Everything that lives and moves will be food for you. Just as I gave you the green plants, I now give you everything.

Psalm 17

14 You still the hunger of those you cherish; their sons have plenty, and they store up wealth for their children.

Psalm 23

1 The Lord is my shepherd, I shall lack nothing. 2 He makes me lie down in green pastures, He leads me beside quiet waters, 3 He restores my soul. He guides me in paths of righteousness for His name's sake.

Psalm 34

9 Fear the Lord, you His saints, for those who fear him lack nothing. 10 The lions may grow weak and

hungry, but those who seek the Lord lack no good thing.

Psalm 37

25 I was young and now I am old, yet I have never seen the righteous forsaken or their children begging bread. 26 They are always generous and lend freely; their children will be blessed.

Psalm 107

9 For He satisfies the thirsty and fills the hungry with good things.

Psalm 111

5 He provides food for those who fear Him; He remembers his covenant forever.

Psalm 127

2 In vain you rise early and stay up late, toiling for food to eat—for He grants sleep to those He loves.

Psalm 136

25 He gives food to every living thing, for His lovingkindness continues forever (TLB).

Matthew 6

7,8 Don't recite the same prayer over and over as the heathen do, who think prayers are answered only by repeating them again and again. Remember, your Father knows exactly what you need even before you ask Him! (TLB).

25 Therefore I tell you, do not worry about your life, what you will eat or drink; or about your body, what you will wear. Is not life more important than food, and the body more important than clothes? 26 Look at the birds of the air; they do not sow or reap or store away in barns, and yet your heavenly Father feeds them. Are you not much more valuable than they? 27 Who of you by worrying can add a single hour to his life? 28 And why do you worry about clothes? See how the lilies of the field grow.

They do not labor or spin. 29 Yet I tell you that not even Solomon in all his splendor was dressed like one of these. 30 If that is how God clothes the grass of the field, which is here today and tomorrow is thrown into the fire, will He not much more clothe you, O you of little faith? 31 So do not worry, saying, "What shall we eat?" or "What shall we drink?" or "What shall we wear?" 32 For the pagans run after all these things, and your heavenly Father knows that you need them. 33 But seek first His kingdom and His righteousness, and all these things will be given to you as well. 34 Therefore do not worry about tomorrow, for tomorrow will worry about itself. Each day has enough trouble of its own [also found in Luke 12:22–31].

Matthew 16

8 Aware of their discussion, Jesus asked, "You of little faith, why are you talking among yourselves about having no bread? 9 Do you still not understand? Don't you remember the five loaves for the five thousand, and how many basketfuls you gathered? 10 Or the seven loaves for the four thousand, and how many basketfuls you gathered?

Philippians 4

19 And my God will meet all your needs according to his glorious riches in Christ Jesus.

1 Timothy 5

3 Give proper recognition to those widows who are really in need. 4 But if a widow has children or grandchildren, these should learn first of all to put their religion into practice by caring for their own family and so repaying their parents and grandparents, for this is pleasing to God. 5 The widow who is really in need and left all alone puts her hope in God and continues night and day to pray and to ask God for help.

8 If anyone does not provide for his relatives, and especially for his immediate family, he has denied the faith and is worse than an unbeliever.

Responding to the NEEDY
(See also Needs, Sharing)

Leviticus 19

9 When you reap the harvest of your land, do not reap to the very edges of your field or gather the gleanings of your harvest. 10 Do not go over your vineyard a second time or pick up the grapes that have fallen. Leave them for the poor and the alien. I am the Lord your God.

Deuteronomy 15

10 Give generously to him [a poor man] and do so without a grudging heart; then because of this the Lord your God will bless you in all your work and in everything you put your hand to. 11 There will always be poor people in the land. Therefore I command you to be openhanded toward your brothers and toward the poor and needy in your land.

Job 31

16 If I have denied the desires of the poor or let the eyes of the widow grow weary, 17 if I have kept my bread to myself, not sharing it with the fatherless— 18 but from my youth I reared him as would a father, and from my birth I guided the widow— 19 if I have seen anyone perish for lack of clothing, or a needy man without a garment, 20 and his heart did not bless me for warming him with the fleece from my sheep, 21 if I have raised my hand against the fatherless, knowing that I had

influence in court, then let my arm fall from the shoulder, let it be broken off at the joint.

Proverbs 14

20 Even his own neighbors despise the poor man, while the rich have many "friends." 21 To despise the poor is to sin. Blessed are those who pity them (TLB).

Proverbs 19

17 He who is kind to the poor lends to the Lord, and He will reward him for what he has done.

Proverbs 22

9 A generous man will himself be blessed, for he shares his food with the poor.

Proverbs 28

27 He who gives to the poor will lack nothing, but he who closes his eyes to them receives many curses.

Isaiah 58

7 I want you to share your food with the hungry and bring right into your own homes those who are helpless, poor and destitute. Clothe those who are cold and don't hide from relatives who need your help (TLB).

10 Feed the hungry! Help those in trouble! Then your light will shine out from the darkness, and the darkness around you shall be as bright as day. 11 And the Lord will guide you continually, and satisfy you with all good things, and keep you healthy too; and you will be like a well-watered garden, like an ever-flowing spring (TLB).

Matthew 6

1 Be careful not to do your "acts of righteousness" before men, to be seen by them. If you do, you will have no reward from your Father in heaven. 2 So when you give to the needy, do not announce it with trumpets, as the hypocrites do in the syna-

gogues and on the streets, to be honored by men. I tell you the truth, they have received their reward in full. 3 But when you give to the needy, do not let your left hand know what your right hand is doing, 4 so that your giving may be in secret. Then your Father, who sees what is done in secret, will reward you.

Luke 12

33 Sell your possessions and give to the poor. Provide purses for yourselves that will not wear out, a treasure in heaven that will not be exhausted, where no thief comes near and no moth destroys.

Luke 14

12 Then Jesus said to his host, "When you give a luncheon or dinner, do not invite your friends, your brothers or relatives, or your rich neighbors; if you do, they may invite you back and so you will be repaid. 13 But when you give a banquet, invite the poor, the crippled, the lame, the blind, 14 and you will be blessed. Although they cannot repay you, you will be repaid at the resurrection of the righteous."

1 Timothy 5

3 Give proper recognition to those widows who are really in need. 4 But if a widow has children or grandchildren, these should learn first of all to put their religion into practice by caring for their own family and so repaying their parents and grandparents, for this is pleasing to God. 5 The widow who is really in need and left all alone puts her hope in God and continues night and day to pray and to ask God for help.

James 1

27 Religion that God our Father accepts as pure and faultless is this: to look after orphans and widows in their distress and to keep oneself from being polluted by the world.

James 2

14 What good is it, my brothers, if a man claims to have faith but has no deeds? Can such faith save him? 15 Suppose a brother or sister is without clothes and daily food. 16 If one of you says to him, "Go, I wish you well; keep warm and well fed," but does nothing about his physical needs, what good is it?

1 John 3

16 This is how we know what love is: Jesus Christ laid down His life for us. And we ought to lay down our lives for our brothers. 17 If anyone has material possessions and sees his brother in need but has no pity on him, how can the love of God be in him? 18 Dear children, let us not love with words or tongue but with actions and in truth. 19 This then is how we know that we belong to the truth, and how we set our hearts at rest in His presence.

Understanding
OWNERSHIP
(See also Stewardship)

Genesis 1

1 In the beginning God created the heavens and the earth.

Genesis 2

7 And the Lord God formed man from the dust of the ground and breathed into his nostrils the breath of life, and man became a living being.

Deuteronomy 10

14 To the Lord your God belong the heavens, even the highest heavens, the earth and everything in it.

1 Chronicles 29

11 Yours, O Lord, is the greatness and the power and the glory and the majesty and the splendor, for everything in heaven and earth is Yours. Yours, O Lord, is the kingdom; You are exalted as head over all. 12 Wealth and honor come from You; You are the ruler of all things. In Your hands are strength and power to exalt and give strength to all.

Job 1

21 Naked I came from my mother's womb, and naked I will depart. The Lord gave and the Lord has taken away; may the name of the Lord be praised.

Job 41

11 Who has a claim against Me that I must pay? Everything under heaven belongs to Me.

Psalm 24

1 The earth is the Lord's, and everything in it, the world, and all who live in it; 2 for He founded it upon the seas and established it upon the waters [also found in 1 Corinthians 10:26].

Psalm 50

10 For every animal of the forest is Mine, and the cattle on a thousand hills. 11 I know every bird in the mountains, and the creatures of the field are Mine. 12 If I were hungry I would not tell you, for the world is Mine, and all that is in it.

Psalm 100

3 Know that the Lord is God. It is He who made us, and we are His; we are His people, the sheep of His pasture.

Psalm 103

19 The Lord has established His throne in heaven, and His kingdom rules over all.

Haggai 2

8 "The silver is Mine and the gold is Mine," declares the Lord Almighty.

John 1

1 In the beginning was the Word, and the Word was with God, and the Word was God. 2 He was with God in the beginning. 3 Through Him all things were made; without Him nothing was made that has been made.

John 3

27 A man can receive only what is given him from heaven.

Acts 17

24 The God who made the world and everything in it is the Lord of heaven and earth and does not live in temples built by hands. 25 And He is not served by human hands, as if He needed anything, because He himself gives all men life and breath and everything else. 26 From one man He made every nation of men, that they should inhabit the whole earth; and He determined the times set for them and the exact places where they should live. 27 God did this so that men would seek Him and perhaps reach out for Him and find Him, though He is not far from each one of us. 28 "For in Him we live and move and have our being." As some of your own poets have said, "We are His offspring."

Romans 11

35 "Who has ever given to God, that God should repay him?" 36 For from Him and through Him and to Him are all things. To Him be the glory forever! Amen.

1 Corinthians 4

7 For who makes you different from anyone else? What do you have that you did not receive? And if you did receive it, why do you boast as though you did not?

The Principles of
PARTNERSHIPS
(See also Business Practices, Unity)

Deuteronomy 22

9 Do not plant two kinds of seed in your vineyard; if you do, not only the crops you plant but also the fruit of the vineyard will be defiled. 10 Do not plow with an ox and a donkey yoked together. 11 Do not wear clothes of wool and linen woven together.

Proverbs 22

24 Do not make friends with a hot-tempered man, do not associate with one easily angered, 25 or you may learn his ways and get yourself ensnared.

Proverbs 27

17 As iron sharpens iron, so one man sharpens another.

Ecclesiastes 4

9 Two are better than one, because they have a good return for their work: 10 If one falls down, his friend can help him up. But pity the man who falls and has no one to help him up!

Isaiah 30

1 Woe to My rebellious children, says the Lord: you ask advice from everyone but Me, and decide to

do what I don't want you to do. You yoke yourselves
with unbelievers, thus piling up your sins (TLB).

Amos 3

3 Do two walk together, unless they be agreed to
do so?

2 Corinthians 6

14 Do not be yoked together with unbelievers. For
what do righteousness and wickedness have in common? Or what fellowship can light have with darkness? 15 What harmony is there between Christ
and Belial? What does a believer have in common
with an unbeliever? 16 What agreement is there between the temple of God and idols? For we are the
temple of the living God. As God has said: "I will
live with them and walk among them, and I will be
their God, and they will be My people.
17 Therefore come out from them and be separate,"
says the Lord.

Ephesians 5

6 Let no one deceive you with empty words, for
because of such things God's wrath comes on those
who are disobedient. 7 Therefore do not be part-
ners with them.

Practicing
PATIENCE
(See also Contentment, Greed, Prudence)

Psalm 27

14 Wait for the Lord; be strong and take heart and wait for the Lord.

Psalm 37

5 Commit your way to the Lord; trust in Him and He will do this: 6 He will make your righteousness shine like the dawn, the justice of your cause like the noonday sun. 7 Be still before the Lord and wait patiently for Him; do not fret when men succeed in their ways, when they carry out their wicked schemes.

34 Wait for the Lord and keep His way.

Psalm 40

1 I waited patiently for the Lord; He turned to me and heard my cry. 2 He lifted me out of the slimy pit, out of the mud and mire; He set my feet on a rock and gave me a firm place to stand.

Proverbs 14

29 A patient man has great understanding.

Proverbs 19

11 A man's wisdom gives him patience.

Proverbs 25

15 Through patience a ruler can be persuaded, and a gentle tongue can break a bone.

Ecclesiastes 7

8 The end of a matter is better than its beginning, and patience is better than pride.

PLANNING
From God's Perspective
(See also Budgeting)

Psalm 1

6 For the Lord watches over all the plans and paths of godly men, but the paths of the godless lead to doom (TLB).

Psalm 127

1 Unless the Lord builds the house, its builders labor in vain.

Proverbs 12

20 Deceit fills hearts that are plotting for evil; joy fills hearts that are planning for good! (TLB)

Proverbs 13

16 A wise man thinks ahead; a fool doesn't, and even brags about it!(TLB)

Proverbs 16

1 We can make our plans, but the final outcome is in God's hands (TLB).

3 Commit to the Lord whatever you do, and your plans will succeed.

9 In his heart a man plans his course, but the Lord determines his steps.

Proverbs 19

21 Many are the plans in a man's heart, but it is the Lord's purpose that prevails.

Proverbs 21

30 There is no wisdom, no insight, no plan that can succeed against the Lord.

Proverbs 24

3 By wisdom a house is built, and through understanding it is established; 4 through knowledge its rooms are filled with rare and beautiful treasures.

3,4 Any enterprise is built by wise planning, becomes strong through common sense, and profits wonderfully by keeping abreast of the facts (TLB).

27 Finish your outdoor work and get your fields ready; after that, build your house.

Proverbs 27

1 Do not boast about tomorrow, for you do not know what a day may bring forth.

Jeremiah 29

11 "For I know the plans I have for you," declares the Lord, "plans to prosper you and not to harm you, plans to give you hope and a future. 12 Then you will call upon Me and come and pray to Me, and I will listen to you. 13 You will seek Me and find Me when you seek Me with all your heart."

Lamentations 3

40 Let us examine our ways and test them, and let us return to the Lord.

Luke 14

28 Suppose one of you wants to build a tower. Will he not first sit down and estimate the cost to see if he has enough money to complete it? 29 For if he lays the foundation and is not able to finish it, everyone who sees it will ridicule him, 30 saying, "This fellow began to build and was not able to finish."

1 Corinthians 14

40 But everything should be done in a fitting and orderly way.

James 4

13 Now listen, you who say, "Today or tomorrow we will go to this or that city, spend a year there, carry on business and make money." 14 Why, you do not even know what will happen tomorrow. What is your life? You are a mist that appears for a little while and then vanishes. 15 Instead, you ought to say, "If it is the Lord's will, we will live and do this or that." 16 As it is, you boast and brag. All such boasting is evil. 17 Anyone, then, who knows the good he ought to do and doesn't do it, sins.

Dealing with
PRIDE
(See also Attitude)

Deuteronomy 8

11 Be careful that you do not forget the Lord your God, failing to observe His commands, His laws and His decrees that I am giving you this day. 12 Otherwise, when you eat and are satisfied, when you build fine houses and settle down, 13 and when your herds and flocks grow large and your silver and gold increase and all you have is multiplied, 14 then your heart will become proud and you will forget the Lord your God.

17 You may say to yourself, "My power and the strength of my hands have produced this wealth for me." 18 But remember the Lord your God, for it is He who gives you the ability to produce wealth.

Psalm 10

2 In his arrogance the wicked man hunts down the weak, who are caught in the schemes he devises. 3 He boasts of the cravings of his heart; he blesses the greedy and reviles the Lord. 4 In his pride the wicked does not seek him; in all his thoughts there is no room for God.

Psalm 138

6 Though the Lord is on high, He looks upon the lowly, but the proud He knows from afar.

Proverbs 15

25 The Lord tears down the proud man's house but He keeps the widow's boundaries intact.

Proverbs 16

5 The Lord detests all the proud of heart. Be sure of this: They will not go unpunished.

18 Pride goes before destruction, a haughty spirit before a fall. 19 Better to be lowly in spirit and among the oppressed than to share plunder with the proud.

Proverbs 22

4 Humility and the fear of the Lord bring wealth and honor and life.

Proverbs 26

12 Do you see a man wise in his own eyes? There is more hope for a fool than for him.

Jeremiah 9

23 This is what the Lord says: "Let not the wise man boast of his wisdom or the strong man boast of his strength or the rich man boast of his riches, 24 but let him who boasts boast about this: that he understands and knows Me, that I am the Lord, who exercises kindness, justice and righteousness on earth, for in these I delight," declares the Lord.

Matthew 23

11 The greatest among you will be your servant. 12 For whoever exalts himself will be humbled, and whoever humbles himself will be exalted [also found in Luke 14:11 and 18:14b].

Romans 12

16 Live in harmony with one another. Do not be proud, but be willing to associate with people of low position. Do not be conceited.

1 Corinthians 4

7 For who makes you different from anyone else? What do you have that you did not receive? And if you did receive it, why do you boast as though you did not?

2 Corinthians 10

17 "Let him who boasts boast in the Lord." 18 For it is not the man who commends himself who is approved, but the man whom the Lord commends.

Galatians 6

2 Carry each other's burdens, and in this way you will fulfill the law of Christ. 3 If anyone thinks he is something when he is nothing, he deceives himself. 4 Each one should test his own actions. Then he can take pride in himself, without comparing himself to somebody else, 5 for each one should carry his own load.

1 Timothy 6

17 Command those who are rich in this present world not to be arrogant nor to put their hope in wealth, which is so uncertain, but to put their hope in God who richly provides us with everything for our enjoyment. 18 Command them to do good, to be rich in good deeds, and to be generous and willing to share. 19 In this way they will lay up treasure for themselves as a firm foundation for the coming age, so that they may take hold of the life that is truly life.

James 1

9 The brother in humble circumstances ought to take pride in his high position. 10 But the one who is rich should take pride in his low position, because he will pass away like a wild flower. 11 For the sun rises with scorching heat and withers the plant; its blossom falls and its beauty is destroyed. In the same

way, the rich man will fade away even while he goes about his business.

Revelation 3

17 You say, "I am rich; I have acquired wealth and do not need a thing." But you do not realize that you are wretched, pitiful, poor, blind and naked. 18 I counsel you to buy from Me gold refined in the fire, so you can become rich; and white clothes to wear, so you can cover your shameful nakedness; and salve to put on your eyes, so you can see.

Applying
PRUDENCE
in Decision Making
(See also Patience, Wisdom)

Proverbs 8

12 I, wisdom, dwell together with prudence; I possess knowledge and discretion.

Proverbs 12

23 A prudent man keeps his knowledge to himself, but the heart of fools blurts out folly.

Proverbs 13

16 Every prudent man acts out of knowledge, but a fool exposes his folly.

Proverbs 14

8 The wisdom of the prudent is to give thought to their ways, but the folly of fools is deception.

15 A simple man believes anything, but a prudent man gives thought to his steps.

18 The simple inherit folly, but the prudent are crowned with knowledge.

Proverbs 15

5 A fool spurns his father's discipline, but whoever heeds correction shows prudence.

Proverbs 18

13 What a shame—yes, how stupid!—to decide before knowing the facts! (TLB)

15 The heart of the discerning acquires knowledge; the ears of the wise seek it out.

Proverbs 19

2 It is not good to have zeal without knowledge, nor to be hasty and miss the way.

8 He who gets wisdom loves his own soul; he who cherishes understanding prospers.

Proverbs 22

3 A prudent man foresees the difficulties ahead and prepares for them; the simpleton goes blindly on and suffers the consequences (TLB).

Proverbs 27

12 The prudent see danger and take refuge, but the simple keep going and suffer for it.

Long Life and
RETIREMENT
(See also Planning, Savings)

Psalm 92

12 The righteous will flourish like a palm tree,
they will grow like a cedar of Lebanon;
13 planted in the house of the Lord, they will flourish in the courts of our God. 14 They will still bear
fruit in old age, they will stay fresh and green,
15 proclaiming, "The Lord is upright; He is my
Rock, and there is no wickedness in Him."

Proverbs 6

6 Go to the ant, you sluggard; consider its ways
and be wise! 7 It has no commander, no overseer or
ruler, 8 yet it stores its provisions in summer and
gathers its food at harvest.

Proverbs 9

11 For through me [wisdom] your days will be
many, and years will be added to your life.
12 If you are wise, your wisdom will reward you; if
you are a mocker, you alone will suffer.

Proverbs 10

5 He who gathers crops in summer is a wise son,
but he who sleeps during harvest is a disgraceful
son.

27 The fear of the Lord adds length to life, but the
years of the wicked are cut short. 28 The prospect

of the righteous is joy, but the hopes of the wicked come to nothing. 29 The way of the Lord is a refuge for the righteous, but it is the ruin of those who do evil. 30 The righteous will never be uprooted, but the wicked will not remain in the land.

Proverbs 16

31 Gray hair is a crown of splendor; it is attained by a righteous life.

Proverbs 21

20 In the house of the wise are stores of choice food and oil, but a foolish man devours all he has.

20 The wise man saves for the future, but the foolish man spends whatever he gets (TLB).

Proverbs 28

16 He who hates ill-gotten gain will enjoy a long life.

Proverbs 30

25 Ants are creatures of little strength, yet they store up their food in the summer.

Ecclesiastes 5

13,14 There is another serious problem I have seen everywhere—savings are put into risky investments that turn sour, and soon there is nothing left to pass on to one's son. 15 The man who speculates is soon back to where he began—with nothing. 16 This, as I said, is a very serious problem, for all his hard work has been for nothing; he has been working for the wind. It is all swept away. 17 All the rest of his life he is under a cloud—gloomy, discouraged, frustrated, and angry (TLB).

Ecclesiastes 11

7 It is a wonderful thing to be alive! 8 If a person lives to be very old, let him rejoice in every day of life (TLB).

Isaiah 46

4 Even to your old age and gray hairs I am He, I am He who will sustain you. I have made you and I will carry you; I will sustain you and I will rescue you.

The Rewards of RIGHTEOUSNESS
(See also Honesty)

Deuteronomy 6

18 Do what is right and good in the Lord's sight, so that it may go well with you.

2 Chronicles 16

9 For the eyes of the Lord range throughout the earth to strengthen those whose hearts are fully committed to him.

Job 27

16 Though he [the wicked man] heaps up silver like dust and clothes like piles of clay, 17 what he lays up the righteous will wear, and the innocent will divide his silver. 18 The house he builds is like a moth's cocoon, like a hut made by a watchman. 19 He lies down wealthy, but will do so no more; when he opens his eyes, all is gone.

Psalm 37

25 I was young and now I am old, yet I have never seen the righteous forsaken or their children begging bread. 26 They are always generous and lend freely; their children will be blessed.

Proverbs 4

11 I would have you learn this great fact: that a life of doing right is the wisest life there is (TLB).

23 Above all else, guard your heart, for it is the wellspring of life.

Proverbs 10

16 The wages of the righteous bring them life, but the income of the wicked brings them punishment.

Proverbs 11

4 Your riches won't help you on Judgement Day; only righteousness counts then (TLB).

16 A kindhearted woman gains respect, but ruthless men gain only wealth. 17 A kind man benefits himself, but a cruel man brings himself harm. 18 The wicked man earns deceptive wages, but he who sows righteousness reaps a sure reward.

28 Whoever trusts in his riches will fall, but the righteous will thrive like a green leaf.

Proverbs 13

21 Misfortune pursues the sinner, but prosperity is the reward of the righteous.

22 A good man leaves an inheritance for his children's children, but a sinner's wealth is stored up for the righteous.

Proverbs 15

6 The house of the righteous contains great treasure, but the income of the wicked brings them trouble.

Proverbs 21

21 He who pursues righteousness and love finds life, prosperity and honor.

Proverbs 22

1 A good name is more desirable than great riches; to be esteemed is better than silver or gold.

Isaiah 33

15 He who walks righteously and speaks what is right, who rejects gain from extortion and keeps his

hand from accepting bribes, who stops his ears against plots of murder and shuts his eyes against contemplating evil—this is the man who will dwell on the heights; whose refuge will be the mountain fortress. His bread will be supplied, and water will not fail him.

Matthew 5

6 Blessed are those who hunger and thirst for righteousness, for they will be filled [also found in Luke 6:21a].

Matthew 6

1 Be careful not to do your "acts of righteousness" before men, to be seen by them. If you do, you will have no reward from your Father in heaven. 2 So when you give to the needy, do not announce it with trumpets, as the hypocrites do in the synagogues and on the streets, to be honored by men. I tell you the truth, they have received their reward in full. 3 But when you give to the needy, do not let your left hand know what your right hand is doing, 4 so that your giving may be in secret. Then your Father, who sees what is done in secret, will reward you.

What God Says About
SAVINGS
(See also Investing, Wealth)

Proverbs 6

6 Go to the ant, you sluggard; consider its ways and be wise! 7 It has no commander, no overseer or ruler, 8 yet it stores its provisions in summer and gathers its food at harvest.

Proverbs 13

11 Dishonest money dwindles away, but he who gathers money little by little makes it grow.

Proverbs 19

11 A man's wisdom gives him patience.

Proverbs 21

20 In the house of the wise are stores of choice food and oil, but a foolish man devours all he has.

20 The wise man saves for the future, but the foolish man spends whatever he gets (TLB).

Proverbs 22

3 A prudent man foresees the difficulties ahead and prepares for them; the simpleton goes blindly on and suffers the consequences (TLB).

Proverbs 30

25 Ants are creatures of little strength, yet they store up their food in the summer.

Ecclesiastes 5

13,14 There is another serious problem I have seen everywhere—savings are put into risky investments that turn sour, and soon there is nothing left to pass on to one's son (TLB).

Where to Find
SECURITY

2 Samuel 22

2 The Lord is my rock, my fortress and my deliverer; 3 my God is my rock, in whom I take refuge, my shield and the horn of my salvation. He is my stronghold, my refuge and my savior.

Job 31

24 If I have put my trust in gold or said to pure gold, "You are my security," 25 if I have rejoiced over my great wealth, the fortune my hands had gained, 26 if I have regarded the sun in its radiance or the moon moving in splendor, 27 so that my heart was secretly enticed and my hand offered them a kiss of homage, 28 then these also would be sins to be judged, for I would have been unfaithful to God on high.

Psalm 16

5 Lord, You have assigned me my portion and my cup; You have made my lot secure.

Psalm 23

1 The Lord is my shepherd, I shall lack nothing. 2 He makes me lie down in green pastures, He leads me beside quiet waters, 3 He restores my soul. He guides me in paths of righteousness for His name's sake.

Psalm 37

23 The Lord delights in the way of the man whose steps He has made firm; 24 though he stumble, he

will not fall, for the Lord upholds him with his hand.

27 Turn from evil and do good; then you will always live securely. 28 For the Lord loves the just and will not forsake His faithful ones. They will be protected forever, but the offspring of the wicked will be cut off; 29 the righteous will inherit the land and dwell in it forever.

39 The salvation of the righteous comes from the Lord; He is their stronghold in time of trouble. 40 The Lord helps them and delivers them; He delivers them from the wicked and saves them, because they take refuge in Him.

Psalm 121

5 The Lord watches over you—the Lord is your shade at your right hand; 6 the sun will not harm you by day, nor the moon by night. 7 The Lord will keep you from all harm—He will watch over your life; 8 the Lord will watch over your coming and going both now and forevermore.

Proverbs 3

5 Trust in the Lord with all your heart and lean not on your own understanding; 6 in all your ways acknowledge Him, and He will make your paths straight.

25 Have no fear of sudden disaster or of the ruin that overtakes the wicked, 26 for the Lord will be your confidence and will keep your foot from being snared.

Isaiah 33

6 He will be the sure foundation for your times, a rich store of salvation and wisdom and knowledge; the fear of the Lord is the key to this treasure.

Isaiah 40

28 Do you not know? Have you not heard? The Lord is the everlasting God, the Creator of the ends of the earth. He will not grow tired or weary, and

His understanding no one can fathom. 29 He gives strength to the weary and increases the power of the weak. 30 Even youths grow tired and weary, and young men stumble and fall; 31 but those who hope in the Lord will renew their strength. They will soar on wings like eagles; they will run and not grow weary, they will walk and not be faint.

Matthew 11

28 Come to Me, all you who are weary and burdened, and I will give you rest. 29 Take My yoke upon you and learn from Me, for I am gentle and humble in heart, and you will find rest for your souls. 30 For My yoke is easy and My burden is light.

Luke 6

46 Why do you call Me, "Lord, Lord," and do not do what I say? 47 I will show you what he is like who comes to Me and hears My words and puts them into practice. 48 He is like a man building a house, who dug down deep and laid the foundation on rock. When a flood came, the torrent struck that house but could not shake it, because it was well built. 49 But the one who hears My words and does not put them into practice is like a man who built a house on the ground without a foundation. The moment the torrent struck that house, it collapsed and its destruction was complete [also found in Matthew 7:24–27].

John 10

27 My sheep listen to My voice; I know them, and they follow Me. 28 I give them eternal life, and they shall never perish; no one can snatch them out of My hand.

Romans 8

31 If God is for us, who can be against us?

38 For I am convinced that neither death nor life,

neither angels nor demons, neither the present nor the future, nor any powers, 39 neither height nor depth, nor anything else in all creation, will be able to separate us from the love of God that is in Christ Jesus our Lord.

2 Timothy 1

12 I know whom I have believed, and am convinced that He is able to guard what I have entrusted to Him for that day.

SHARING
God's Way
(See also Giving, Needy)

Psalm 37

25 I was young and now I am old, yet I have never seen the righteous forsaken or their children begging bread. 26 They are always generous and lend freely; their children will be blessed.

Ecclesiastes 11

1 Cast your bread upon the waters, for after many days you will find it again.

Isaiah 58

7 I want you to share your food with the hungry and bring right into your own homes those who are helpless, poor and destitute. Clothe those who are cold and don't hide from relatives who need your help (TLB).

Matthew 25

34 Then the King will say to those on His right, "Come, you who are blessed by My Father; take your inheritance, the kingdom prepared for you since the creation of the world. 35 For I was hungry and you gave Me something to eat, I was thirsty and you gave Me something to drink, I was a stranger and you invited Me in, 36 I needed clothes and you clothed Me, I was sick and you looked after Me, I was in prison and you came to visit Me." 37 Then the righteous will answer him, "Lord, when did we see You hungry and feed You, or thirst

and give You something to drink? 38 When did we
see You a stranger and invite You in, or needing
clothes and clothe You? 39 When did we see You
sick or in prison and go to visit You?"
40 The King will reply, "I tell you the truth, whatever you did for one of the least of these brothers of
Mine, you did for Me" [also found in Matthew 25:42
–46].

Mark 9

41 I tell you the truth, anyone who gives you a
cup of water in My name because you belong to
Christ will certainly not lose his reward.

Luke 3

11 The man with two tunics should share with
him who has none, and the one who has food
should do the same.

Luke 6

38 Give, and it will be given to you. A good measure, pressed down, shaken together and running
over, will be poured into your lap. For with the measure you use, it will be measured to you.

Luke 10

30 Jesus said: "A man was going down from
Jerusalem to Jericho, when he fell into the hands of
robbers. They stripped him of his clothes, beat him
and went away, leaving him half dead.
31 A priest happened to be going down the same
road, and when he saw the man, he passed by on
the other side. 32 So too, a Levite, when he came to
the place and saw him, passed by on the other side.
33 But a Samaritan, as he traveled, came where the
man was; and when he saw him, he took pity on
him. 34 He went to him and bandaged his wounds,
pouring on oil and wine. Then he put the man on his
own donkey, took him to an inn and took care of
him. 35 The next day he took out two silver coins
and gave them to the innkeeper. 'Look after him,' he
said, 'and when I return, I will reimburse you for

any extra expense you may have.' 36 Which of these three do you think was a neighbor to the man who fell into the hands of robbers?" 37 The expert in the law replied, "The one who had mercy on him." Jesus told him, "Go and do likewise."

Acts 4

32 All the believers were one in heart and mind. No one claimed that any of his possessions was his own, but they shared everything they had. 33 With great power the apostles continued to testify to the resurrection of the Lord Jesus, and much grace was with them all. 34 There were no needy persons among them. For from time to time those who owned lands or houses sold them, brought the money from the sales 35 and put it at the apostles' feet, and it was distributed to anyone as he had need.

Acts 20

33 I [Paul] have not coveted anyone's silver or gold or clothing. 34 You yourselves know that these hands of mine have supplied my own needs and the needs of my companions. 35 In everything I did, I showed you that by this kind of hard work we must help the weak, remembering the words the Lord Jesus Himself said: "It is more blessed to give than to receive."

Romans 12

13 Share with God's people who are in need. Practice hospitality.

2 Corinthians 8

12 For if the willingness is there, the gift is acceptable according to what one has, not according to what he does not have. 13 Our desire is not that others might be relieved while you are hard pressed, but that there might be equality. 14 At the present time your plenty will supply what they need, so that in turn their plenty will supply what you need. Then there will be equality, 15 as it is written: "He that

gathered much did not have too much, and he that gathered little did not have too little."

Galantians 6

2 Carry each other's burdens, and in this way you will fulfill the law of Christ. 3 If anyone thinks he is something when he is nothing, he deceives himself. 4 Each one should test his own actions. Then he can take pride in himself, without comparing himself to somebody else, 5 for each one should carry his own load.

9 Let us not become weary in doing good, for at the proper time we will reap a harvest if we do not give up. 10 Therefore, as we have opportunity, let us do good to all people, especially to those who belong to the family of believers.

Ephesians 4

28 He who has been stealing must steal no longer, but must work, doing something useful with his own hands, that he may have something to share with those in need.

Hebrews 6

10 God is not unjust; He will not forget your work and the love you have shown Him as you have helped His people and continue to help them.

Hebrews 13

2 Do not forget to entertain strangers, for by so doing some people have entertained angels without knowing it.

16 And do not forget to do good and to share with others, for with such sacrifices God is pleased.

1 Peter 4

9 Offer hospitality to one another without grumbling.

Your Responsibility Toward STEWARDSHIP
(See also Budgeting, Giving, Ownership, Planning)

Genesis 1

27 So God created man in His own image, in the image of God He created him; male and female He created them. 28 God blessed them and said to them, "Be fruitful and increase in number; fill the earth and subdue it. Rule over the fish of the sea and the birds of the air and over every living creature that moves on the ground."

Deuteronomy 11

13 So if you faithfully obey the commands I am giving you today—to love the Lord your God and to serve him with all your heart and with all your soul— 14 then I will send rain on your land in its season, both autumn and spring rains, so that you may gather in your grain, new wine and oil. 15 I will provide grass in the field for your cattle, and you will eat and be satisfied.

Joshua 24

15 But if serving the Lord seems undesirable to you, then choose for yourselves this day whom you will serve, (whether the gods your forefathers served beyond the River, or the gods of the Amorites, in whose land you are living.) But as for me and my household, we will serve the Lord.

Psalm 62

11 One thing God has spoken, two things have I heard: that You, O God, are strong, 12 and that You, O Lord, are loving. Surely You will reward each person according to what he has done.

Psalm 115

16 The highest heavens belong to the Lord, but the earth He has given to man.

Psalm 119

90 Your faithfulness continues through all generations; You established the earth, and it endures. 91 Your laws endure to this day, for all things serve You.

Matthew 6

24 No one can serve two masters. Either he will hate the one and love the other, or he will be devoted to the one and despise the other. You cannot serve both God and Money [also found in Luke 16:-13].

Matthew 25

14 Again, it will be like a man going on a journey, who called his servants and entrusted his property to them. 15 To one he gave five talents of money, to another two talents, and to another one talent, each according to his ability. Then he went on his journey. 16 The man who had received the five talents went at once and put his money to work and gained five more. 17 So also, the one with the two talents gained two more. 18 But the man who had received the one talent went off, dug a hole in the ground and hid his master's money. 19 After a long time the master of those servants returned and settled accounts with them. 20 The man who had received the five talents brought the other five. "Master," he said, "you entrusted me with five talents. See, I have gained five more." 21 His master replied, "Well done, good and faithful servant! You

have been faithful with a few things; I will put you in charge of many things. Come and share your master's happiness!" 22 The man with the two talents also came. "Master," he said, "you entrusted me with two talents; see, I have gained two more." 23 His master replied, "Well done, good and faithful servant! You have been faithful with a few things; I will put you in charge of many things. Come and share your master's happiness!" 24 Then the man who had received the one talent came. "Master," he said, "I knew that you are a hard man, harvesting where you have not sown and gathering where you have not scattered seed. 25 So I was afraid and went out and hid your talent in the ground. See, here is what belongs to you." 26 His master replied, "You wicked, lazy servant! So you knew that I harvest where I have not sown and gather where I have not scattered seed? 27 Well then, you should have put my money on deposit with the bankers, so that when I returned I would have received it back with interest. 28 Take the talent from him and give it to the one who has the ten talents. 29 For everyone who has will be given more, and he will have an abundance. Whoever does not have, even what he has will be taken from him. 30 And throw that worthless servant outside, into the darkness, where there will be weeping and gnashing of teeth" [also found in Luke 19:12–26].

Luke 12

48 From everyone who has been given much, much will be demanded; and from the one who has been entrusted with much, much more will be asked.

Luke 16

10 Whoever can be trusted with very little can also be trusted with much, and whoever is dishonest with very little will also be dishonest with much. 11 So if you have not been trustworthy in handling worldly wealth, who will trust you with true riches? 12 And if you have not been trustworthy with some-

one else's property, who will give you property of
your own?

Romans 14

12 So then, each of us will give an account of himself to God.

1 Corinthians 3

10 By the grace God has given me, I laid a foundation as an expert builder, and someone else is building on it. But each one should be careful how he
builds. 11 For no one can lay any foundation other
than the one already laid, which is Jesus Christ.
12 If any man builds on this foundation using gold,
silver, costly stones, wood, hay or straw,
13 his work will be shown for what it is, because the
Day will bring it to light. It will be revealed with fire,
and the fire will test the quality of each man's work.
14 If what he has built survives, he will receive his
reward. 15 If it is burned up, he will suffer loss; he
himself will be saved, but only as one escaping
through the flames.

1 Corinthians 4

2 Now it is required that those who have been giv-
en a trust must prove faithful

2 Moreover it is required in stewards, that a man
be found faithful (KJV).

2 Corinthians 5

9 So we make it our goal to please Him, whether
we are at home in the body or away from it.
10 For we must all appear before the judgment seat
of Christ, that each one may receive what is due him
for the things done while in the body, whether good
or bad.

Ephesians 2

10 For we are God's workmanship, created in
Christ Jesus to do good works, which God prepared
in advance for us to do.

2 Timothy 2

15 Do your best to present yourself to God as one approved, a workman who does not need to be ashamed and who correctly handles the word of truth.

1 Peter 4

10 Each one should use whatever gift he has received to serve others, faithfully administering God's grace in its various forms.

Achieving True
SUCCESS
(See also Attitude, Security)

Joshua 1

8 Do not let this book of the law depart from your mouth; meditate on it day and night, so that you may be careful to do everything written in it. Then you will be prosperous and successful.

1 Samuel 2

7 The Lord sends poverty and wealth; He humbles and He exalts. 8 He raises the poor from the dust and lifts the needy from the ash heap; He seats them with princes and has them inherit a throne of honor. "For the foundations of the earth are the Lord's; upon them He has set the world."

Psalm 37

11 But all who humble themselves before the Lord shall be given every blessing, and shall have wonderful peace (TLB).

35 I have seen a wicked and ruthless man flourishing like a green tree in its native soil, 36 but he soon passed away and was no more; though I looked for him, he could not be found.

Psalm 128

1 Blessed are all who fear the Lord, who walk in His ways. 2 You will eat the fruit of your labor; blessings and prosperity will be yours. 3 Your wife will be like a fruitful vine within your

house; your sons will be like olive shoots around your table. 4 Thus is the man blessed who fears the Lord.

Proverbs 3

1 My son, do not forget my teaching, but keep my commands in your heart, 2 for they will prolong your life many years and bring you prosperity. 3 Let love and faithfulness never leave you; bind them around your neck, write them on the tablet of your heart. 4 Then you will win favor and a good name in the sight of God and man.

4,5 If you want favor with both God and man, and a reputation for good judgment and common sense, then trust the Lord completely; don't ever trust yourself. 6 In everything you do, put God first, and He will direct you and crown your efforts with success (TLB).

Proverbs 10

30 The good shall never lose God's blessings, but the wicked shall lose everything (TLB).

Proverbs 12

3 Wickedness never brings real success; only the godly have that (TLB).

24 Work hard and become a leader; be lazy and never succeed (TLB).

Proverbs 14

14 The faithless will be fully repaid for their ways, and the good man rewarded for his.

Proverbs 16

20 Whoever gives heed to instruction prospers, and blessed is he who trusts in the Lord.

Proverbs 19

8 He who loves wisdom loves his own best interest and will be a success (TLB).

Proverbs 28

12 When the godly are successful, everyone is glad. When the wicked succeed, everyone is sad (TLB).

13 A man who refuses to admit his mistakes can never be successful. But if he confesses and forsakes them, he gets another chance (TLB).

Ecclesiastes 9

11 I have seen something else under the sun: The race is not to the swift or the battle to the strong, nor does food come to the wise or wealth to the brilliant or favor to the learned; but time and chance happen to them all.

Ecclesiastes 10

10 If the ax is dull and its edge unsharpened, more strength is needed, but skill will bring success.

Jeremiah 17

7 But blessed is the man who trusts in the Lord, whose confidence is in Him. 8 He will be like a tree planted by the water that sends out its roots by the stream. It does not fear when heat comes; its leaves are always green. It has no worries in a year of drought and never fails to bear fruit. 9 The heart is deceitful above all things and beyond cure. Who can understand it? 10 I the Lord search the heart and examine the mind, to reward a man according to his conduct, according to what his deeds deserve.

Matthew 16

26 What good will it be for a man if he gains the whole world, yet forfeits his soul? Or what can a man give in exchange for his soul? [also found in Mark 8:36 and Luke 9:25].

John 10

10 The thief cometh not, but for to steal, and to kill, and to destroy: I am come that they might have

life, and that they might have it more abundantly
(KJV).

1 Corinthians 9

24 Do you not know that in a race all the runners
run, but only one gets the prize? Run in such a way
as to get the prize.   25 Everyone who competes in
the games goes into strict training. They do it to get
a crown that will not last; but we do it to get a crown
that will last forever.   26 Therefore I do not run like
a man running aimlessly; I do not fight like a man
beating the air.

Hebrews 11

6 And without faith it is impossible to please God,
because anyone who comes to Him must believe that
He exists and that He rewards those who earnestly
seek Him.

Your Attitude Toward
TAXES
(See also Honesty,
Righteousness)

Proverbs 28

4 Those who forsake the law praise the wicked, but those who keep the law resist them.

7 He who keeps the law is a discerning son.

9 If anyone turns a deaf ear to the law, even his prayers are detestable.

Luke 20

22 "Is it right for us to pay taxes to Caesar or not?" 23 He saw through their duplicity and said to them, 24 "Show Me a denarius. Whose portrait and inscription are on it?" 25 "Caesar's," they replied. He said to them, "Then give to Caesar what is Caesar's, and to God what is God's" [also found in Matthew 22:17–21 and Mark 12:14–17].

Romans 2

23 You who brag about the law, do you dishonor God by breaking the law?

Romans 13

1 Everyone must submit himself to the governing authorities, for there is no authority except that which God has established. The authorities that exist have been established by God. 2 Consequently, he who rebels against the authority is rebelling against

what God has instituted, and those who do so will bring judgment on themselves. 3 For rulers hold no terror for those who do right, but for those who do wrong. Do you want to be free from fear of the one in authority? Then do what is right and he will commend you. 4 For he is God's servant to do you good. But if you do wrong, be afraid, for he does not bear the sword for nothing. He is God's servant, an agent of wrath to bring punishment on the wrongdoer. 5 Therefore, it is necessary to submit to the authorities not only because of possible punishment but also because of conscience. 6 This is also why you pay taxes, for the authorities are God's servants, who give their full time to governing. 7 Give everyone what you owe him: If you owe taxes, pay taxes; if revenue, then revenue; if respect, then respect; if honor, then honor.

Titus 3

1 Remind the people to be subject to rulers and authorities, to be obedient, to be ready to do whatever is good.

1 Peter 2

13 Submit yourselves for the Lord's sake to every authority instituted among men.

17 Show respect for everyone. Love Christians everywhere. Fear God and honor the government (TLB).

Recognizing Real
TREASURE
(See also Wealth)

Psalm 119

162 I rejoice in Your laws like one who finds a great treasure (TLB).

Psalm 127

3 Children are a gift from God; they are His reward (TLB).

Proverbs 2

3,4,5 Yes, if you want better insight and discernment, and are searching for them as you would for lost money or hidden treasure, then wisdom will be given you, and knowledge of God Himself; you will soon learn the importance of reverence for the Lord and of trusting Him. 6 For the Lord grants wisdom! His every word is a treasure of knowledge and understanding. 7,8 He grants good sense to the godly—His saints. He is their shield, protecting them and guarding their pathway. 9 He shows how to distinguish right from wrong, how to find the right decision every time. 10 For wisdom and truth will enter the very center of your being, filling your life with joy (TLB).

Proverbs 10

2 Ill-gotten treasures are of no value, but righteousness delivers from death.

Proverbs 15

6 The house of the righteous contains great treasure, but the income of the wicked brings them trouble.

Proverbs 24

3 By wisdom a house is built, and through understanding it is established; 4 through knowledge its rooms are filled with rare and beautiful treasures.

Isaiah 33

6 He will be the sure foundation for your times, a rich store of salvation and wisdom and knowledge; the fear of the Lord is the key to this treasure.

Matthew 6

19 Do not store up for yourselves treasures on earth, where moth and rust destroy, and where thieves break in and steal. 20 But store up for yourselves treasures in heaven, where moth and rust do not destroy, and where thieves do not break in and steal. 21 For where your treasure is, there your heart will be also [also found in Luke 12:33–34].

Matthew 19

16 Now a man came up to Jesus and asked, "Teacher, what good thing must I do to get eternal life?" 17 "Why do you ask Me about what is good?" Jesus replied. "There is only One who is good. If you want to enter life, obey the commandments." 18 "Which ones?" the man inquired. Jesus replied, " 'Do not murder, do not commit adultery, do not steal, do not give false testimony, 19 honor your father and mother,' and 'love your neighbor as yourself.' " 20 "All these I have kept," the young man said. "What do I still lack?" 21 Jesus answered, "If you want to be perfect, go, sell you possessions and give to the poor, and you will have treasure in heaven. Then come, follow Me." 22 When the young man heard this, he went away sad, because he had great wealth.

23 Then Jesus said to His disciples, "I tell you the truth, it is hard for a rich man to enter the kingdom of heaven. 24 Again I tell you, it is easier for a camel to go through the eye of a needle than for a rich man to enter the kingdom of God" [also found in Mark 10:17–24, Luke 18:18–25].

Luke 12

33 Sell your possessions and give to the poor. Provide purses for yourselves that will not wear out, a treasure in heaven that will not be exhausted, where no thief comes near and no moth destroys.

Colossians 2

2 My purpose is that they may be encouraged in heart and united in love, so that they may have the full riches of complete understanding, in order that they may know the mystery of God, namely, Christ, 3 in whom are hidden all the treasures of wisdom and knowledge.

1 Timothy 6

17 Command those who are rich in this present world not to be arrogant nor to put their hope in wealth, which is so uncertain, but to put their hope in God who richly provides us with everything for our enjoyment. 18 Command them to do good, to be rich in good deeds, and to be generous and willing to share. 19 In this way they will lay up treasure for themselves as a firm foundation for the coming age, so that they may take hold of the life that is truly life.

The Wisdom of
UNITY
*(See also Counsel—For
Husband and Wife,
Partnerships)*

Genesis 2

23 The man said, "This is now bone of my bones and flesh of my flesh; she shall be called 'woman,' for she was taken out of man." 24 For this reason a man will leave his father and mother and be united to his wife, and they will become one flesh.

Genesis 11

6 The Lord said, "If as one people speaking the same language they have begun to do this, then nothing they plan to do will be impossible for them."

Psalm 133

1 How good and pleasant it is when brothers live together in unity!

Ecclesiastes 4

9 Two are better than one, because they have a good return for their work. 10 If one falls down, his friend can help him up. But pity the man who falls and has no one to help him up! 11 Also, if two lie down together, they will keep warm. But how can one keep warm alone? 12 Though one may be over-powered, two can defend themselves. A cord of three strands is not quickly broken.

Amos 3

3 Do two walk together, unless they be agreed to do so?

Matthew 12

25 Jesus knew their thoughts and said to them, "Every kingdom divided against itself will be ruined, and every city or household divided against itself will not stand."

Matthew 18

19 Again, I tell you that if two of you on earth agree about anything you ask for, it will be done for you by My Father in heaven. 20 For where two or three come together in My name, there am I with them.

John 17

21 My prayer for all of them is that they will be of one heart and mind, just as You and I are, Father—that just as You are in Me and I am in You, so they will be in Us, and the world will believe you sent Me. 22 I have given them the glory You gave Me—the glorious unity of being one, as We are—23 I in them and You in Me, all being perfected into one—so that the world will know You sent Me and will understand that You love them as much as You love Me (TLB).

Acts 2

44 All the believers were together and had everything in common. 45 Selling their possessions and goods, they gave to anyone as he had need.

Acts 4

32 All the believers were one in heart and mind. No one claimed that any of his possessions was his own, but they shared everything they had. 33 With great power the apostles continued to testify to the resurrection of the Lord Jesus, and much grace was with them all. 34 There were no needy

persons among them. For from time to time those who owned lands or houses sold them, brought the money from the sales 35 and put it at the apostles' feet, and it was distributed to anyone as he had need.

Philippians 2

2 Then make my joy complete by being like-minded, having the same love, being one in spirit and purpose.

Colossians 2

2 My purpose is that they may be encouraged in heart and united in love, so that they may have the full riches of complete understanding, in order that they may know the mystery of God, namely, Christ, 3 in whom are hidden all the treasures of wisdom and knowledge.

Understanding True
WEALTH
(See also Money, Treasure)

1 Samuel 2

7 The Lord sends poverty and wealth; He humbles and He exalts. 8 He raises the poor from the dust and lifts the needy from the ash heap; He seats them with princes and has them inherit a throne of honor. "For the foundations of the earth are the Lord's; upon them He has set the world."

Psalm 37

16 Better the little that the righteous have than the wealth of many wicked; 17 for the power of the wicked will be broken, but the Lord upholds the righteous.

Psalm 39

6 Man is a mere phantom as he goes to and fro: He bustles about, but only in vain; he heaps up wealth, not knowing who will get it.

Psalm 49

5 Why should I fear when evil days come, when wicked deceivers surround me— 6 those who trust in their wealth and boast of their great riches? 7 No man can redeem the life of another or give to God a ransom for him— 8 the ransom for a life is costly, no payment is ever enough— 9 that he should live on forever and not see decay. 10 For all can see that wise men die; the foolish and the senseless alike perish and leave their wealth to

others. 11 Their tombs will remain their houses forever, their dwellings for endless generations, though they had named lands after themselves. 12 But man, despite his riches, does not endure; he is like the beasts that perish. 13 This is the fate of those who trust in themselves, and of their followers, who approve their sayings.

Psalm 52

6 The righteous will see and fear; they will laugh at him [a man], saying, 7 "Here now is the man who did not make God his stronghold but trusted in his great wealth and grew strong by destroying others!"

Proverbs 10

15 The rich man's wealth is his only strength. The poor man's poverty is his only curse (TLB).

22 The blessing of the Lord brings wealth, and He adds no trouble to it.

Proverbs 11

18 The evil man gets rich for the moment, but the good man's reward lasts forever (TLB).

Proverbs 13

7 One man pretends to be rich, yet has nothing; another pretends to be poor, yet has great wealth.

Proverbs 15

16 Better a little with the fear of the Lord than great wealth with turmoil. 17 Better a meal of vegetables where there is love than a fattened calf with hatred.

Proverbs 16

16 How much better to get wisdom than gold, to choose understanding rather than silver!

Proverbs 18

11 The rich man thinks of his wealth as an impregnable defense, a high wall of safety. What a dreamer! (TLB)

Proverbs 21

17 He who loves pleasure will become poor; whoever loves wine and oil will never be rich.

Proverbs 23

4 Do not wear yourself out to get rich; have the wisdom to show restraint. 5 Cast but a glance at riches, and they are gone, for they will surely sprout wings and fly off to the sky like an eagle.

Proverbs 28

19 He who works his land will have abundant food, but the one who chases fantasies will have his fill of poverty. 20 A faithful man will be richly blessed, but one eager to get rich will not go unpunished.

Ecclesiastes 2

26 To the man who pleases Him, God gives wisdom, knowledge and happiness, but to the sinner He gives the task of gathering and storing up wealth to hand it over to the one who pleases God. This too is meaningless, a chasing after the wind.

Ecclesiastes 5

19 Moreover, when God gives any man wealth and possessions, and enables him to enjoy them, to accept his lot and be happy in his work—this is a gift of God. 20 He seldom reflects on the days of his life, because God keeps him occupied with gladness of heart.

2 Corinthians 8

9 For you know the grace of our Lord Jesus Christ, that though He was rich, yet for your sakes He

became poor, so that you through His poverty might become rich.

Colossians 3

1 Since, then, you have been raised with Christ, set your hearts on things above, where Christ is seated at the right hand of God. 2 Set your minds on things above, not on earthly things.

James 5

1 Now listen, you rich people, weep and wail because of the misery that is coming upon you. 2 Your wealth has rotted, and moths have eaten your clothes. 3 Your gold and silver are corroded. Their corrosion will testify against you and eat your flesh like fire. You have hoarded wealth in the last days. 4 Look! The wages you failed to pay the workmen who mowed your fields are crying out against you. The cries of the harvesters have reached the ears of the Lord Almighty. 5 You have lived on earth in luxury and self-indulgence. You have fattened yourselves in the day of slaughter.

1 John 2

15 Do not love the world or anything in the world. If anyone loves the world, the love of the Father is not in him. 16 For everything in the world—the cravings of sinful man, the lust of his eyes and the boastings of what he has and does—comes not from the Father but from the world. 17 The world and its desires pass away, but the man who does the will of God lives forever.

Obtaining God's
WISDOM
(See also Prudence)

Job 12

13 To God belong wisdom and power; counsel and understanding are His.

Job 28

12 But where can wisdom be found? Where does understanding dwell? 13 Man does not comprehend its worth; it cannot be found in the land of the living. 14 The deep says, "It is not in me"; the sea says, "It is not with me." 15 It cannot be bought with the finest gold, nor can its price be weighed in silver. 16 It cannot be bought with the gold of Ophir, with precious onyx or sapphires. 17 Neither gold nor crystal can compare with it, nor can it be had for jewels of gold. 18 Coral and jasper are not worthy of mention; the price of wisdom is beyond rubies. 19 The topaz of Cush cannot compare with it; it cannot be bought with pure gold. 20 Where then does wisdom come from? Where does understanding dwell? 21 It is hidden from the eyes of every living thing, concealed even from the birds of the air. 22 Destruction and Death say, "Only a rumor of it has reached our ears." 23 God understands the way to it and He alone knows where it dwells, 24 for He views the ends of the earth and sees everything under the heavens. 25 When He established the force of the wind and measured out the waters, 26 when He made a decree for the rain and a path for the thunderstorm,

27 then He looked at wisdom and appraised it; He confirmed it and tested it. 28 And He said to man, "The fear of the Lord—that is wisdom, and to shun evil is understanding."

Proverbs 3

7 Do not be wise in your own eyes; fear the Lord and shun evil.

13 Blessed is the man who finds wisdom, and the man who gains understanding.

13,14,15 The man who knows right from wrong and has good judgment and common sense is happier than the man who is immensely rich! For such wisdom is far more valuable than precious jewels. Nothing else compares with it. 16,17 Wisdom gives: A long, good life, riches, honor, pleasure, peace. 18 Wisdom is a tree of life to those who eat her fruit; happy is the man who keeps on eating it (TLB).

Proverbs 4

5 Get wisdom, get understanding; do not forget my words or swerve from them. 6 Do not forsake wisdom, and she will protect you; love her, and she will watch over you. 7 Wisdom is supreme; therefore get wisdom. Though it cost all you have, get understanding.

Proverbs 8

17 I [wisdom] love those who love me, and those who seek me find me. 18 With me are riches and honor, enduring wealth and prosperity. 19 My fruit is better than fine gold; what I yield surpasses choice silver. 20 I walk in the way of righteousness, along the paths of justice, 21 bestowing wealth on those who love me and making their treasuries full.

Proverbs 9

10 The fear of the Lord is the beginning of wisdom, and knowledge of the Holy One is understanding.

Proverbs 17

16 Of what use is money in the hand of a fool, since he has no desire to get wisdom?

Proverbs 19

8 He who gets wisdom loves his own soul; he who cherishes understanding prospers.

Proverbs 23

23 Buy the truth and do not sell it; get wisdom, discipline and understanding.

Proverbs 24

3 By wisdom a house is built, and through understanding it is established; 4 through knowledge its rooms are filled with rare and beautiful treasures.

5 A wise man has great power, and a man of knowledge increases strength;

Proverbs 28

11 A rich man may be wise in his own eyes, but a poor man who has discernment sees through him.

Ecclesiastes 7

11 Wisdom, like an inheritance, is a good thing and benefits those who see the sun. 12 Wisdom is a shelter as money is a shelter, but the advantage of knowledge is this: that wisdom preserves the life of its possessor.

Ecclesiastes 8

1 Who is like the wise man? Who knows the explanation of things? Wisdom brightens a man's face and changes its hard appearance.

Ecclesiastes 12

13 Now all has been heard; here is the conclusion of the matter: Fear God and keep His commandments, for this is the whole duty of man.

14 For God will bring every deed into judgment, including every hidden thing, whether it is good or evil.

1 Corinthians 3

18 Do not deceive yourselves. If any one of you thinks he is wise by the standards of this age, he should become a "fool" so that he may become wise. 19 For the wisdom of this world is foolishness in God's sight. As it is written: "He catches the wise in their craftiness"; 20 and again, "The Lord knows that the thoughts of the wise are futile."

Ephesians 5

15 Be very careful, then, how you live—not as unwise but as wise, 16 making the most of every opportunity, because the days are evil. 17 Therefore do not be foolish, but understand what the Lord's will is.

James 1

5 If any of you lacks wisdom, he should ask God, who gives generously to all without finding fault, and it will be given to him. 6 But when he asks, he must believe and not doubt, because he who doubts is like a wave of the sea, blown and tossed by the wind. 7 That man should not think he will receive anything from the Lord; 8 he is a double-minded man, unstable in all he does.

How to Deal With WORRY
(See also Adversity, Security)

Psalm 56

3 When I am afraid, I will trust in You. 4 In God, whose word I praise, in God I trust; I will not be afraid. What can mortal man do to me?

Psalm 94

19 When anxiety was great within me, Your consolation brought joy to my soul.

Psalm 118

24 This is the day the Lord has made; let us rejoice and be glad in it.

Psalm 139

23 Search me, O God, and know my heart; test me and know my anxious thoughts. 24 See if there is any offensive way in me, and lead me in the way everlasting.

Proverbs 12

25 An anxious heart weighs a man down.

Ecclesiastes 5

12 The sleep of a laborer is sweet, whether he eats little or much, but the abundance of a rich man permits him no sleep.

Jeremiah 17

7 But blessed is the man who trusts in the Lord, whose confidence is in Him. 8 He will be like a tree planted by the water that sends out its roots by the stream. It does not fear when heat comes; its leaves are always green. It has no worries in a year of drought and never fails to bear fruit.

Matthew 6

25 Therefore I tell you, do not worry about your life, what you will eat or drink; or about your body, what you will wear. Is not life more important than food, and the body more important than clothes? 26 Look at the birds of the air; they do not sow or reap or store away in barns, and yet your heavenly Father feeds them. Are you not much more valuable than they? 27 Who of you by worrying can add a single hour to his life? 28 And why do you worry about clothes? See how the lilies of the field grow. They do not labor or spin. 29 Yet I tell you that not even Solomon in all his splendor was dressed like one of these. 30 If that is how God clothes the grass of the field, which is here today and tomorrow is thrown into the fire, will He not much more clothe you, O you of little faith? 31 So do not worry, saying, "What shall we eat?" or "What shall we drink?" or "What shall we wear?" 32 For the pagans run after all these things, and your heavenly Father knows that you need them. 33 But seek first His kingdom and His righteousness, and all these things will be given to you as well. 34 Therefore do not worry about tomorrow, for tomorrow will worry about itself. Each day has enough trouble of its own [also found in Luke 12:22–31].

Matthew 10

29 Are not two sparrows sold for a penny? Yet not one of them will fall to the ground apart from the will of your Father. 30 And even the very hairs of your head are all numbered. So don't be afraid; you are worth more than many sparrows [also found in Luke 12:6,7].

Mark 4

18 Still others, like seed sown among thorns, hear the word; 19 but the worries of this life, the deceitfulness of wealth and the desires for other things come in and choke the word, making it unfruitful. 20 Others, like seed sown on good soil, hear the word, accept it, and produce a crop—thirty, sixty or even a hundred times what was sown [also found in Matthew 13:22 and Luke 8:14].

Luke 12

32 Do not be afraid, little flock, for your Father has been pleased to give you the kingdom.

Luke 21

34 Be careful, or your hearts will be weighed down with dissipation, drunkenness and the anxieties of life, and that day will close on you unexpectedly like a trap.

John 14

27 Peace I leave with you; My peace I give you. I do not give to you as the world gives. Do not let your hearts be troubled and do not be afraid.

John 16

33 I have told you these things, so that in Me you may have peace. In this world you will have trouble. But take heart! I have overcome the world.

Philippians 4

6 Do not be anxious about anything, but in everything, by prayer and petition, with thanksgiving, present your requests to God. 7 And the peace of God, which transcends all understanding, will guard your hearts and your minds in Christ Jesus.

Hebrews 13

6 So we say with confidence, "The Lord is my helper; I will not be afraid. What can man do to me?"

1 Peter 5

7 Cast all your anxiety on Him because He cares for you.

Cross Reference Index

Surety—see Cosigning, Debt, Lending
Talents (use of)—see Investing, Labor, Prudence, Savings,
 Stewardship
Theft—see Honesty
Thrift—see Savings
Tithe, tithing—see Giving
Troubles—see Adversity, Security, Worry
Trust (in God)—see Security
Truthfulness—see Honesty, Righteousness
Understanding—see Counsel, Wisdom
Unjust gain—see Honesty
Unselfishness—see Giving, Sharing
Usury—see Lending
Vanity—see Pride
Vocation—see Business Practices, Labor
Wages—see Business Practices, Labor
Wants—see Attitude, Desires
Wastefulness—see Stewardship
Widows—see Needy, Sharing
Wills and trusts—see Needs, Planning, Stewardship
Word (God's)—see Counsel, Wisdom
Work—see Business Practices, Labor
Worldliness—see Attitude, Contentment, Desires, Success
Yield—see Investing, Savings, Stewardship